Lenormand Step by Step

A Course in the Petit Lenormand

Kendra Hurteau

ISBN-13: 978-1792986284
ISBN-10: 1792986284

Copyright © 2018 by Kendra Hurteau

First Edition

All rights reserved. No part of this publication may be reproduced, stored, or transmitted in any way without the prior written permission of the author.

Front cover design by Katrina Hill
Card Layouts, Spreads, and Lists by Kendra Hurteau
http://lenormandcards.wixsite.com/lenormand

Image Disclosure

The images in this book are slightly blurred to protect the integrity of the card decks and copyright of all materials.

Editions

There are two paperback editions of Lenormand Step by Step, a standard pages edition and a color pages edition. The eBook contains color images, as well. This is the standard pages edition.

Acknowledgements

Thank you for your interest in this book and in the Petit Lenormand. I hope you find some treasure in these pages that aid your Lenormand studies.

I want to specifically thank Katrina Hill, Autumn Jeffers, and Liza Shone. They encouraged me, supported my goal to finish Lenormand Step by Step, gave me excellent feedback, and edited my work. Each individual contributed something unique to this book. It became what it is because of them. I am truly grateful for these ladies.

Table of Contents

About the Author	1
Our Work	4
Chapter 1: Introduction to Lenormand	12
A Short Lenormand History	12
The Mystery in Lenormand	14
Approach	15
Reading Method	17
Reading Guidelines	19
Chapter 2: Language of Lenormand	22
Terminology	22
Pronunciation	27
Chapter 3: Step 1: Keywords	28
The Steps	28
Create Keywords	29
Suggested Keywords	36
PAM List	39
Chapter 4: Step 2: Combinations	41
Step 2: Combinations	41
Single Cards	41
2 Card Combinations	42
People in the Cards	50
Work in the Cards	53
Money Cards	54
Intimate Relationships	56
Opposing Cards	57
Posing Questions	58
Yes/No Answers	59

Table of Contents Continued

Chapter 5: Step 3: Card Lines — 62
- Step 3: Card Lines — 62
- 3 Card Line — 62
  - Method 1 — 63
  - Method 2 — 64
  - Method 3 — 65
  - Method 4 — 67
- Card Clusters — 68
- 5 Card Line — 72
- Lenormand and Tarot Side by Side Readings — 77

Chapter 6: Step 4: 9 Card Square — 79
- Step 4: 9 Card Square — 79
- 9 Card Square Format — 81
- The 9 Card Square Quick Reference Guide — 87
- 11 Card Spread — 89
- Other Medium-Sized Spreads — 90

Chapter 7: Step 5: Petit Tableau — 95
- Step 5: Petit Tableau — 95
- Petit Tableau Format — 97
- The Petit Tableau Quick Reference Guide — 106

Chapter 8: Step 6: Grand Tableau — 108
- Step 6: The Grand Tableaus — 108
- Advanced Techniques — 118
- Nuances — 123
- The Grand Tableau Quick Reference Guide — 131

Chapter 9: Step 7: Suggestions — 133

Appendix — 138
Bibliography

About the Author

Welcome to Lenormand Step by Step!

My name is Kendra Hurteau. Like you, I study the card divination system known as the Petit Lenormand. Like the lessons that follow, my personal journey with the Petit Lenormand system was a series of steps that led to the writing of this book. In addition, I have created five Lenormand decks and a video course. I trust my direct method of teaching Lenormand will help you read the system with ease and efficiency.

My Story

In 2005, while involved in other esoteric studies, I delved into the world of Tarot. I was active in The Detroit Area Tarot Guild and that is where I first laid eyes on a Lenormand Grand Tableau. In that very viewing of the thirty-six Lenormand cards, I knew I would make a deck of my own. I spent hours of each day immersed in the system, learning where it came from and how it works. I then combined my efforts with Katrina Hill, an artist and graphic designer, to create our first deck. We wanted an Edwardian feel to it and so the images in Under the Roses represent that era. Katrina, who is also my daughter, ultimately illustrated four of our five decks.

Readings by Kendra

I read for clients in person, online, and by phone. My readings are practical and down-to-earth, yet empathic and intuitive. I use divination tools such as the Lenormand, Tarot, pendulums, and stones. It is easy to schedule a reading with me at:
https://kendrakh.appointy.com/default.aspx
Please email me your name and contact information at kendra.hurteau@gmail.com if there are any issues with scheduling.

Our Work

Under the Roses Lenormand

Katrina and I initially self-published Under the Roses Lenormand in 2012. U.S. Games Systems, Inc. later published the deck in 2015.

The allusion "under the roses" dates back to Roman times and it implies there are hidden secrets. People would say that things were "buried under the roses." In this day and age, a similar idiom is "behind closed doors." The deck backs are roses, implying that the secrets are underneath. In addition, we incorporated specific rose color meanings throughout the deck. For instance, the blue roses symbolize something that is unattainable or impossible. The yellow roses symbolize friendship. The white roses symbolize sympathy and spirituality. And, naturally, the red roses symbolize love.

Under the Roses Lenormand was the first Petit Lenormand to have keywords on the face of the cards (in the title area as well as the background). Though beginners loved it, many of the more experienced users of Lenormand didn't prefer it that way. So, we issued our second edition both with and without keywords in the title area. To this day we get requests for the cards with keywords, but we no longer control the printing. However, the keywords remain in the background of the images.

Katrina and I were encouraged by the amount of positive feedback we received when we shared Under the Roses Lenormand. That led us to developing our other decks.

Under the Roses Lenormand can be found in stores, online at Amazon, or through U.S. Games Systems, Inc.

Images from Under the Roses Lenormand used with permission of U.S. Games Systems, Stamford, CT 06902 c. 2015 by U.S. Games Systems, Inc. All rights reserved.

Under the Roses Lenormand App

Under the Roses Lenormand is now available as an app. It is a great bargain, so check it out! It can be found through app stores and online through The Fool's Dog.

Halloween Lenormand

Our spoof deck titled "Halloween Lenormand" (a Lenormand Oracle spin-off) was a hit. It was the first holiday-themed Lenormand deck ever sold. The system of Lenormand is very direct and serious, but we wanted to have some fun with it. We want you to laugh when you see it. Initially, I didn't think people would understand it, but I've been pleasantly surprised that so many people perceive the humor in the deck.

Halloween Lenormand can be found online at The Game Crafter.

Yuletide Lenormand

Our third deck, "Yuletide Lenormand," was made right after Halloween Lenormand. It is a quaint Christmastime Lenormand Oracle. I don't think this little gem gets enough attention because it lacks the word "Christmas" in the title. It's delightful and warm. Sometimes I take it out mid-year just to see it again. To this day, it's my favorite Lenormand Oracle.

The deck has a few alternate cards (cards that can be used in lieu of other cards). For instance, the Ring can be replaced by the Wreath and the Lady can be replaced by the Snowlady.

Yuletide Lenormand can be found online at The Game Crafter.

Kendra's Vintage Petit Lenormand

In 2013, I explored how I would create a deck of my own. I love ephemera and wanted a deck with original images that did not contain clipart. Initially, I had planned to print it for myself alone. However, when I began sharing images, my colleagues encouraged me to again self-publish.

Kendra's Vintage Petit Lenormand was issued with four cards numbered 37. Those cards represent subject matters that aren't normally in a Lenormand deck. People who preserve the use of the traditional thirty-six cards can easily take the extras out.

Kendra's Vintage Petit Lenormand is available as a bridge size deck and a mini deck which can be found online at The Game Crafter.

Lenormand Silhouettes

Because I wanted a deck that was elegant and direct, Lenormand Silhouettes was born. This deck is a traditional user's dream. The images are uncluttered and easy to identify. This deck is perfect for those who prefer the clear images the Lenormand cards are known for.

Images from this deck are used frequently in this book.

Lenormand Silhouettes is available as a bridge size deck and a mini deck that can be found online at The Game Crafter.

Lenormand Step by Step:
A Crash Course in the Petit Lenormand

Lenormand Step by Step
A Crash Course in the Petit Lenormand

Naturally, my involvement with Lenormand includes presentations and teaching. Because of that, "Lenormand Step by Step: A Crash Course in the Petit Lenormand Oracle" was developed. Lenormand Step by Step, or LSxS for short, is an online course consisting of seven short videos and an invitation to join a closed Facebook group. The total viewing time is less than two hours and the videos may be watched at any pace. The members are also encouraged to contribute to threads and participate in the group. The goal of the course is to get members reading the Grand Tableau with ease and efficiency.

This instruction manual is an elaboration of the video course. If you are interested in connecting the book and the videos, join us online. Lenormand Step by Step: A Crash Course in the Petit Lenormand can be found at: http://lenormandcards.wixsite.com/lenormand/course

Other Pursuits

Katrina and I both paint fine art. If you would like to follow our work, though our current art endeavors are not related to Lenormand, you can find our projects online at:
https://www.katrinakayart.wixsite.com/katrinakayart
https://kendrafineart.wixsite.com/kendra

Chapter 1: Introduction to Lenormand

A Short Lenormand History

The Petit Lenormand, a thirty-six card deck, was first published in 1846. This card system is based on a previous set of emblematical cards and coffee ground meanings (similar to tea leave readings).

The Petit Lenormand was likely modeled after the *Das Spiel der Hofnung* (aka *The Game of Hope*). *The Game of Hope* was a German game which included a card deck with French suits. It was published circa 1800. Images of the original deck are viewable online at the British Museum.

Very interestingly, there may be a forerunner to the *Game of Hope* that was published in 1796. Tarot author, Mary Greer, has found an older deck that she calls "The Viennese Coffee-Cards" in The British Museum archives. The Viennese Coffee-Cards are a British fortune-telling deck that was published in London and sold for three shillings. The deck was originally titled *The Diversions of The Court of Vienna, in which the Mystery of Fortune-Telling is Unravelled, by Means of Thirty-Two Emblematical Cards, with a Book of Suitable Directions.* It contains most of the images of the Petit Lenormand with a few exceptions. This card deck is also viewable online at the British Museum.

While we will be studying the Petit Lenormand, there are actually two "Lenormand" decks; the Grand Jeu de Mlle. Le Normand (aka Astro Mythological Lenormand) and the Petit Lenormand. The decks are very different and not interchangeable because of their images and card counts. The Grand Jeu Lenormand, a fifty-four card deck, was issued in 1845 in France.

Both of the Lenormand decks were named after an infamous card reader and sibyl named Mademoiselle Marie Anne Adelaide Lenormand. She was born in 1772 and died in France in 1843. Mlle. Lenormand did not actually use either of the Lenormand decks. Instead, she used the Petit Etteilla, Tarot, and playing cards in her readings. She used astrology and other forms of divination as well. Mlle. Lenormand authored several books between 1814 and 1833. Her gifts were considered a "black art" and she was imprisoned for short periods though she maintained a large clientele.

She claimed to have given readings to people like Empress Josephine and Tsar Alexander I.

The Mystery in Lenormand

The Petit Lenormand is like a puzzle. Once a puzzle is assembled, it creates a clear image. The placement of the cards determines how they are viewed and relate to each other.

Lenormand readings are like mysteries to be unraveled. Every reading tells a story we must interpret. We make deductions and derive conclusions. Who is the main character? What is causing their actions? What are they worried about? Is someone else hurting them? Haunting them? Loving them? What prompted them to get a reading? Are they partnered? A parent? A business person? All answers that the cards are more than happy to divulge through observation. Each card is a clue and it is affected by the cards/clues next to it. Then, by observing the reading as a whole, the mystery is revealed.

Approach

For those of you that say "I've tried to read Lenormand, but I just don't get it," I encourage you to continue reading. If you are analytical, use deductive reasoning, or simply enjoy doing puzzles, you will be able to use the Petit Lenormand. This system is also good for people who think they can't read Tarot because they lack the intuition they believe they need.

Because the seasoned Tarot reader is used to Tarot methods, it is actually more difficult to teach them the Lenormand system than a novice reader. They know to search for a story, use their intuition, and put things together in a magical way. They have practiced their talent and studied the suits. None of that applies at the beginning of your Lenormand lessons. However, when approaching Lenormand with a fresh perspective, understanding typically comes quickly.

In any form of card divination, there are several different reading styles. Some people rely on book interpretations and there are those who do not. Some people base their readings on what they know while others base their readings on what they feel. We are all individuals; therefore we all have a different perspective when using the cards.

This course is a blend of traditional Lenormand methods and my own experience of what works. I have added my own techniques throughout the book. However, you are welcome to use the system in the strictest sense.

Some Lenormand readers use their intuition while others don't. Should you choose to add your personal intuition to your Lenormand interpretations then, that is your choice. It is card divination, after all.

When using Lenormand, my preference is to make assessments and deductions first, then use my intuition after that. When using Tarot, I use my intuition first and then apply all I know about the Tarot cards.

Like the Tarot, Lenormand is expanding and evolving. The two systems can both be created with different themes. Other Oracle decks are not cloned in that way. Tarot has evolved as a result of people designing themed and/or modern decks. There is some debate about modifying Lenormand decks in that way. The argument is that the Lenormand system is a set of symbols and changing those symbols could muddle readings or compromise what constitutes it as a Lenormand deck. As a result, some people want to hold onto the original methods exclusively. Still, some would say they want to see Lenormand explored, expanded, and improved upon.

So, why read with Lenormand? Lenormand is more analytical than Tarot. Like Lenormand, Tarot addresses subjects from a deep and philosophical stance. Lenormand may talk about things in one's everyday life as well. This makes it a very useful divination tool. So, be prepared to be surprised and wowed.

Reading Method

Lenormand is a system that requires a method of use, though variations of the art exist. This is *my* method of teaching the Petit Lenormand Oracle. It is based on traditional methods but has a non-traditional start with slight modifications. It is a way to produce clear and detailed readings in a timely manner.
I've heard new Lenormand readers accuse Lenormand of being "boring" or that they don't really "get it." This

may be a simple matter of perspective. There is an expectation to get something magical out of the Lenormand cards, but the cards can offer something more practical.

In this course, our objective is to be able to read any Lenormand layout with ease and accuracy. Therefore, it's imperative, as you follow this course, that you thoroughly understand the lesson you are working on before going to the next. The first few lessons, which cover foundational information, would be lost by skimming or skipping them. By the time we get farther into the lessons and use larger layouts, it becomes clear how the lessons have built on each other. Practice each lesson until you are comfortable. This will save time later when we study spreads. And… enjoy the process along the way!

Lenormand functions differently than other card systems. Like Tarot, it was initially designed as a game. This game, however, is played more deductively than others typically are. Lenormand requires the use of a semantical method, whereby the use of words and their placement are very important to creating a reading.

We will not be studying Tarot in this book, though it is often referenced in a way a novice Lenormand student can understand. Because of the sheer volume of Tarot readers who are interested in Lenormand, this generates a lot of discussion about the two decks systems. I've incorporated that experience into the pages of this book.

Reading Guidelines

When you start a reading, take a moment to ground yourself to clear out unwanted energy. Let life outside the reading area be just that… life outside. By being present and focused, the reading will be clearer.

I cannot stress enough how important your intentions are during the reading process. In addition, make sure that you are in a clear space and not angry, grieving, fearful, stressed, or expecting a particular outcome.

A commonly used guideline for people learning to read the cards is to avoid reading the three D's – Divorce, Disaster, and Death. That is a good starting place. However, also evaluate your own ethics and decide what, in addition, is or is not acceptable.

Use common sense. If you think you see something that may be potentially dreadful for the person receiving the reading, keep it to yourself and let them live without fear. You affect their experience. Providing grim or frightful readings does not help anyone. Even in the midst of tragedy or upset, something positive can happen or new actions can be taken. Try to leave every person with some sort of positive outcome and/or help them see a new perspective. You may make a lasting impact in the life of the person sitting in front of you. Encourage people. They are looking to you for hope.

Third party readings are not advisable. Do not read about someone without them directly granting you expressed consent. "Expressed consent" is when a person directly tells you that you may read for them. This means that if a querent comes to you and wants you to do a reading for or about their boyfriend, child, relative, friend, or business acquaintance you do not have the proper permission to do that. In this instance, you could ethically read how that third person's life or actions affect the person you are reading for. There is a fine line here, but there is a definite line.

The querent may get lost in the Lenormand reading process. So, take a good look at them in the first few minutes of the reading. They are the catalyst for what you'll see in the cards. What are their eyes saying? Does that match what their mouth is saying? Are they uptight? Crying? Dressed well? Are they engaged in the reading? If not, take a minute to get them involved in what they are seeing. Explain to them that they are the main character (Significator). Ask them if they recognize any of the cards as being relevant in their life, because they may see things that they personally identify with.

If you are already an advanced reader, the cards may seem repetitious at times. Look for a fresh message in every reading because each one is unique. Figure out something you hadn't before. You may be surprised by what is there.

Chapter 2: Language of Lenormand

Terminology

A list of commonly confused terms follows.

Flanking Cards
The cards positioned to the left and right of a particular card noted or examined.

Focus Card
A single card that represents the main subject, topic, issue, or situation for which the querent needs clarity.

Influencing
There are areas/lines in the spreads that are described as "influencing." As we explore the bigger layouts, there will be influencing situations to read in the spreads.

Intention
A clear plan of action with a goal of a positive outcome. Intending to use or define the cards in a deliberate way. An attitude of being ethical and clear while using the cards with a specific aim.

Lenormand, Lenormand Oracle, and Lenoracle
- "Lenormand" is the Petit Lenormand deck (sometimes affectionately called "Lennies") that is a distinct set of thirty-six cards which are read in a particular way.
- A "Lenormand Oracle" has come to mean a set of cards similar to Lenormand containing similar images and/or minor additions that still use Lenormand-like methods of interpretation.
- "Lenoracle" was recently coined on the internet. The cards in this type of deck will contain Lenormand symbols but may have many revisions. A Lenoracle is usually read more loosely than Lenormand, sometimes changing the reading process altogether.

Open Reading
A reading that is not prompted by a question. The subject, situation, or issue is found in the reading itself and the reading progresses from there.

Oracle Cards
The word "Oracle" sometimes confuses people. They may assume that an Oracle deck is a deck that is not Tarot or Lenormand. However, all decks used for card

divination are Oracle decks. Tarot is an Oracle system. Lenormand is an Oracle system. Other Oracle decks are independent systems and they are not re-themed or cloned. Those decks are what are typically referred to as "Oracle cards."

PAM
The acronym PAM stands for personally ascribed meaning. PAMs are meanings created in lieu of suggested or traditional meanings of the cards.

Querent
The person the reading is for, whether it be the reader or another person.

Reader
The person divining the cards.

Significator
The main card in question. The main character. The Significator card usually indicates the person receiving the reading. Lenormand has specific Significator cards - the Lady and the Gentleman.

Tableau
The word "tableau" originates from the French language in which the word is defined as a table or board. It is also defined as a scene, painting, picture or arrangement. In the Lenormand system, a tableau is a particular style of reading spread. For our use, I will define a tableau as an arrangement of a collaborative grouping of cards that represent a whole picture.

Traditional
There are two ways you may hear the word "traditional" used in the Lenormand system.
- There is a "traditional" method by which we use Lenormand. The *way* the cards are read together is very important. Otherwise, you wouldn't be reading it as a Lenormand deck; you'd be reading it as an Oracle deck.
- The other way the word "traditional" is used is to describe the use of traditional keywords. These keyword lists, also known as "schools," come from different areas in Europe and are preset lists of particular words used to interpret the cards. Some examples of the "schools" are French, Belgian, German, etc. Petit Lenormand cards were printed with similar or identical meanings

for over two hundred years. It's only been in the last few decades that meanings have been modified to reflect our modern lifestyles.

Pronunciation

Lenormand   \ˈle-nȯrmənd \

There is some debate about how the word "Lenormand" is pronounced. Like other words, including names, pronunciation depends on the geographical area and the origin of the language spoken.

Mlle. Lenormand was French. In the French language, the name describes a descendant of the Normans or a native from Normandy.

The following Lenormand pronunciations are the most commonly used: The English "Len-nor-mand" or "Len-ner-mand" is how it is often spoken in the United States. The French pronunciations "Lu-nor-mah" or "Le-nor-mah" are also widely used. Other pronunciations include "Len-ar-man" and the German "Lee-nor-maund." Because I am American, I prefer to pronounce it "Len-nor-mand."

Chapter 3: Step 1: Keywords

The Steps

In the lessons that follow, we will be using a method in which each lesson builds upon the last. It's important not to jump ahead because doing so will likely affect the accuracy of your readings.

Consider creating a hard companion notebook for your studies. A ring binder works well. There will be several items you may want to collect along the way. Of course, we are living in the digital era, so computer files may be sufficient to meet your needs. The notebook may be as informal as a journal or as organized as a study guide. Include areas for notes, images, print-outs, and lists. Further suggestions are listed in Chapter 9.

Step 1: Create Keywords

This is the first foundational Step in building Lenormand card interpretations. In this chapter, we will determine what each card means.

If the cards are upside down then flip them right-side up. Reversals are not used in Lenormand readings (unlike Tarot).

Get comfortable with the deck by taking a good look at each card. Do not try and interpret the cards at this time.

Each card face image has an emblematical representation or symbol of something or someone on it. The emblem/symbol should stand out. There may be background scenery or imagery, but it is not relevant. The card will also likely contain a card number, card title, and a suit designation, such as the 6♦, which we will use in this course.

We will be using a method of creating keywords known as "personally ascribed meanings," aka "PAMs." By using keywords you have personally designated, it will be easy to identify the meaning of a card and make sense of what you are seeing. Think of it as though you are customizing the deck specifically for yourself.

While PAMs are not considered traditional, they are commonly used. If you wish to use a specific school/traditional list of keywords, such as the French list of keywords, the internet is a good source. Some instructors even keep lists available on their websites. In addition, any decks you purchase should come with a set of keywords that you can use as well. As an example, the Keywords for Lenormand Silhouettes is visible on our website at: http://lenormandcards.wixsite.com/lenormand/keywords In addition, many published card decks have free downloadable little white books (LWBs). Our own Under the Roses Lenormand has a free booklet available through the U.S. Games Systems, Inc. website.

Figure 3a

Almost all of the keywords will be one-word representations of the card you are working with. In this way we choose keywords for each of the cards. Let's use the Clover as an example (Figure 3a). What does it represent to you? When you pull the number 2 card (the Clover) from the deck, do not create a story about what the card may mean. Look at it and think about what a clover represents. Most people will say something like "luck." Maybe it's wishing? Maybe it's money? Again, do not try to read or create an intuitive story about what you see in the individual cards.

List the cards from 1 to 36 and include their titles (see PAMs list at the end of this chapter). Evaluate each card and then write one to three keywords for that card. Use a pencil because you may want to change your keywords later. Don't get too hung up on this list because this is really about your intention for the cards. If you are struggling to find a keyword for any particular card, borrow one from the Suggested Keywords list (at the end of this chapter) until you find your own. You may even use that list in its entirety until you form your own list. Make sure to get familiar with whatever keywords you use before continuing to Step 2.

Both the Gentleman and the Lady have been filled out for you in the PAMs list. You are, of course, welcome to add or change these keywords. These two cards are simply symbols of the querent and someone important to them, such as a significant other.

The cards can take on a literal interpretation as well. The Dog can be a dog, the House can be a house, the Tree can be a tree, etc. The Bouquet might actually be a bundle of flowers that you see in a reading. Because of this, there is no need to add literal interpretations to your PAMs list.

If you would like to make a more thorough list of PAMs you may include nouns, adjectives, and verbs for each card. Personally, I don't do this. I like to keep my list as succinct as possible.

It will later be beneficial to decide which cards have negative, positive, and neutral attributes. Make a notation next to your keywords. It helps if you have a similar amount of each attribute. For instance, you could assign twelve negative cards, twelve positive cards, and twelve neutral cards. The reason behind this will become clearer later in the next chapter. Of course, you can always allow your impression of the card to dictate its quality and not be concerned about balancing attributes.

There are cards that may end up making you cringe when you see them. The usual ones are the Mountain, the Cross, the Mice, or the Snake. Over time they will become very distinct. It is beneficial to remind yourself these cards also have positive attributes and consider listing them.

Return to your PAMs list at a later time to see if the keywords still resonate with you. If, at any time, you revise any, set your intention to match so that the next time you shuffle and pull the cards there won't be any confusion.

Over time, after you are more accustomed to the cards, you may find that the meanings of particular cards seem to be morphing. If this is the case, you have two options. If you want to accept the meaning that has surfaced on its own then revise your PAMs list so that the card now has this new meaning. This is how I finally accepted the keyword "nemesis" for the Snake. If you don't like the meaning the card seems to be projecting, reject that meaning and continue with the keywords that you are comfortable with right now.

Homework:

Make a flashcard game of it. State the first thing you think of when you see the image. This will help you define your keywords and help you understand how the cards work. Give yourself one minute to flash through the deck. It is fun to get others involved and observe what they come up with.

Write a list of your keywords.

Start a notebook for your Lenormand studies. It will be a valuable resource where you will be able to log your keywords, readings, and observations. The Under the Roses Lenormand App has a useful tool for saving your readings, as well.

Suggested Keywords

1 Rider
News, Messenger, Visitor
2 Clover
Luck, Opportunities, Fortune
3 Ship
Travel, Moving, Vehicle
4 House
Home, Family, Property
5 Tree
Growth, Health, Longevity
6 Clouds
Unclear, Doubt, Depression
7 Snake
Betrayal, Seduction, Nemesis
8 Coffin
Transformation, Grief, Loss
9 Bouquet
Abundance, Gift, Romance
10 Scythe
Cut off, Ending, Harvest
11 Whip
Repetition, Arguments, Chemistry
12 Birds
Conversation, Chatter, Pairing
13 Child
Youth, Fun, Child, Sibling
14 Fox
Logic, Intelligence, Cunning
15 Bear
Overbearing, Heavy, Sturdy

16 Stars
Connectedness, Vision, Multitude

17 Stork
Beginning, Momentous Occasion, Announcement

18 Dog
Loyalty, Friendship, Pet

19 Tower
Perspective, Authority, Structure

20 Garden
Gathering, Networking, Event

21 Mountain
Challenge, Blockage, Endurance

22 Crossroads
Choice, Impasse, Direction

23 Mice
Annoyance, Problems, Anxiety

24 Heart
Love, Endearment, Empathy

25 Ring
Commitment, Agreement, Union

26 Book
Secrets, History, Reflection

27 Letter
Correspondence, Contract, Results

28 Man
Querent, Another Person, Important Person

29 Lady
Querent, Another Person, Important Person

30 Lilies
Harmony, Wisdom, Experience

31 Sun
Success, Vitality, Warmth

32 Moon
Cycles, Emotions, Shadowy

33 Key
Answers, Threshold, Destiny

34 Fish
Increase, Indulgences, Wishes

35 Anchor
Stability, Goals, Perseverance

36 Cross
Burdens, Stuck, Hopeless

© Kendra Hurteau 2018

PAMs

(Write your own keywords for each of the cards listed below)

1 Rider
2 Clover
3 Ship
4 House
5 Tree
6 Clouds
7 Snake
8 Coffin
9 Bouquet
10 Scythe
11 Whip
12 Birds
13 Child
14 Fox
15 Bear
16 Stars
17 Stork
18 Dog
19 Tower
20 Garden
21 Mountain
22 Crossroads
23 Mice
24 Heart
25 Ring
26 Book
27 Letter
28 Man - Querent, Significant Other
29 Lady - Querent, Significant Other

30 Lilies
31 Sun
32 Moon
33 Key
34 Fish
35 Anchor
36 Cross

© Kendra Hurteau 2018

Chapter 4: Step 2: Combinations

Step 2: Card Combinations

In this chapter, we will learn how to properly combine cards and gain an understanding of how the Lenormand system works. By using combinations, you will be creating your first Lenormand readings.

Single Cards

Lenormand cards are not read individually; do not pull a card from a Lenormand deck and try and interpret it. There are few exceptions to the rule which are covered later, such as yes/no answers and an advanced method called "houses."

If you are a Tarot reader, you will be accustomed to single card readings. So, the idea that combinations are necessary will be an adjustment until you understand how the cards are paired.

2 Card Combinations

It is imperative that you understand how to use 2 Card Combinations. *All* Petit Lenormand readings are built upon this method of combining the cards.

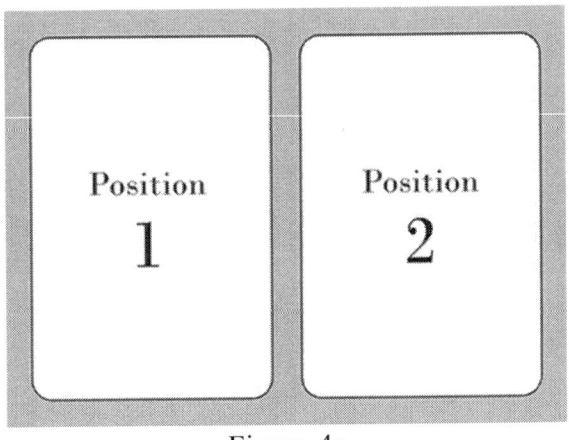

Figure 4a

Position 1 of the combination (Figure 4a) will be the subject or topic of the reading. However, it isn't considered complete without the card in position 2.

Figure 4b

Let's say you have pulled the only the Gentleman in position 1 (Figure 4b). You are only looking at the first card of a combination until the second card is pulled to describe it. So first, by using your keywords, decide what the subject is of the card in position 1 (in this case it is simply a man in question).

Position 2 is a description or enhancement of position 1. Pull the second card and, using your keywords, add a description. Let's say the second card you have pulled is the Dog. If you have chosen "loyal" as a keyword for it, the subject of the reading would not be "loyalty" because that card is in the second position.

Since the first card is the Gentleman, the second card might imply "a loyal man" or "a friend." If using the literal description of the cards, it might make this a man with a dog or a veterinarian.

Figure 4c

Here we have the Crossroads and the Mice (Figure 4c). In this example, we've given the Crossroads the keyword "decision" and the Mice the keyword "annoyance" (these may not be your keywords). "Annoyance" will not be the subject, but the description; "decision" is the subject. If reading it in that order, this would be an annoying decision(s). If I elect to use my other keyword for Mice, "problematic," this would then turn the 2 Card Combination into a "problematic decision(s)."

There is no need to stick to just one keyword (as I have done above) if you have more listed. Find the keyword(s) in your list that makes the most sense to you when you see it.

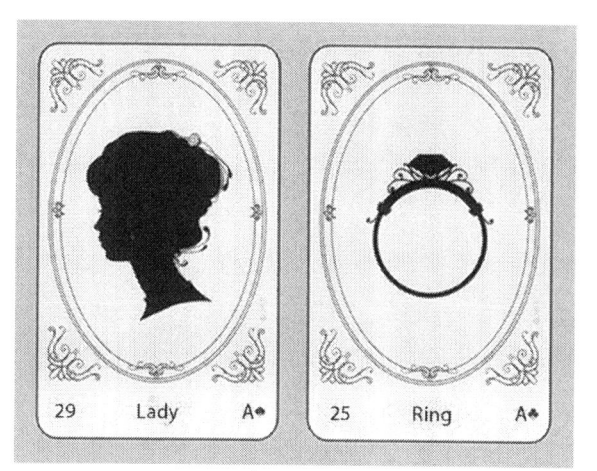

Figure 4d

In another example, say you have decided the keyword for the Ring is "commitment" and the keyword for the Lady, is a Lady. With the Lady in position 1, we know the subject of the reading is a person (Figure 4d). To describe that person, we might say she's a committed lady.

Figure 4e

If the card positions are reversed (Figure 4e), the same reasoning described earlier applies. The reading would not be describing the Lady, it would be describing commitment. So, perhaps the Ring and the Lady may mean that the Lady is getting a commitment she wants? Or that maybe the querent is taking on a new commitment to a person of interest? This is because the main subject is about the commitment itself.

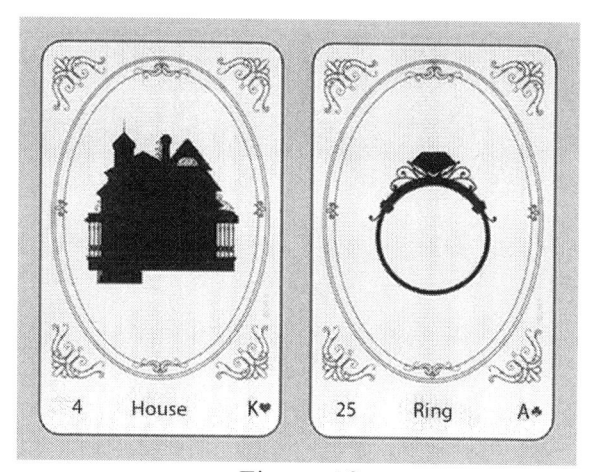

Figure 4f

In a combination of the House and the Ring, the House is the subject (Figure 4f). In the Suggested Keywords list, the House may represent a home or family. With the Ring next to it, the reading would indicate a dedicated family or maybe a home that requires commitment such as a B&B or a home that's been passed down in the family. Maybe the home was purchased after a marriage.

Figure 4g

If the cards are switched around, putting the Ring in the first position (Figure 4g), then the reading becomes about a commitment. The House is describing the commitment, but the Ring is the actual subject. This reading might be talking about a new commitment that must be accomplished for the family. Or a commitment to saving for a home? Or, maybe, a new roommate agreement taking place?

If you understand the system so far and want to make a more thorough list for pairings, then write a list for combinations. Starting with the Rider, list thirty-six possible combinations for each of the cards. For example:

The Rider
(1+1) Rider + Rider =
(1+2) Rider + Clover =
(1+3) Rider + Ship =
(1+4) Rider + House =
Etc.

Make the list for each of the cards. So, the next card is the Clover.

The Clover
(2+1) Clover + Rider =
(2+2) Clover + Clover =
(2+3) Clover + Ship =
(2+4) Clover + House =
Etc.

Following are some random examples for the Tower:
(19+2) Tower + Clover = Casino
(19+9) Tower + Bouquet = Florist
(19+36) Tower + Cross = Hospital or Church

People in the Cards

The Lady, Gentleman, and Child are not necessarily the only cards that represent people in the deck, though they continue to be the primary focus in readings.

To prevent wondering who a card could represent in the middle of a reading, create a list of cards that describe people. Following, are cards commonly used as people in the traditional Lenormand systems. The descriptions are my own. Discard any suggestion that doesn't work for you and add your own ideas if you like. If there is someone in your life that reminds you of a specific card, be sure to add that card to the list. For instance, someone energetic or successful might be represented by the Sun.

- The Rider – This card may represent someone new coming on the scene. I've also seen it surface when a querent has emotions for more than one person.
- The Snake – This card is often seen as "the other woman." Though, in my experience, when the querent doesn't recognize it as some sort of troublemaker or nemesis it is often the querent themselves. We can be our own worst enemy,

and people who are very self-critical or knowingly being unethical may show up as the Snake.
- The Child – A young person, childhood friend, or sibling.
- The Fox – This card can represent someone very crafty or intellectual. Don't underestimate this person; they know what they're up to!
- The Bear – This card often represents a parent, sometimes an overbearing parent. For the most part, I've seen the card represent a mother figure, though it has shown up as a father on occasion. It has that mama-bear-protecting-her-cubs feeling.
- The Stork – An infant or toddler.
- The Dog – A friend, familiar, or pet.
- The Gentleman – A man or person who identifies as such.
- The Lady – A woman or person who identifies as such.
- The Lilies – An older person, a grandparent, or someone experienced.

There are some set traditions as to which cards represent people. The most common is to use the card correspondences that have court cards (jacks, queens, or kings) as identifiers. They are as follows:

J♠ Child
J♥ Heart
J♣ Whip
J♦ Scythe
Q♠ Bouquet
Q♥ Stork
Q♣ Snake
Q♦ Crossroads/Path
K♠ Lilies
K♥ House
K♣ Clouds
K♦ Fish

While some of these cards make sense, many of the cards listed do not make good representations of people. As a result, it is common to see the above list only partially used. If you do use the court card method, I suggest you find a solid source in a traditional Lenormand study in which the cards are specifically designated to represent character archetypes.

Tarot users might be inclined to use the correspondences on Lenormand cards to represent the court cards in the Tarot deck. I strongly urge against that. Because the Lenormand system is not Tarot, the suits are irrelevant. So, the spades don't represent swords, the hearts don't represent cups, the clubs don't represent wands, and the diamonds don't represent pentacles. So, why then, would the card correspondences represent Tarot archetypes?

Work in the Cards

These four cards represent the most common types of careers found in the Lenormand deck. Once you familiarize yourself with them, they can deliver a clear representation of the querent's work life.
- The Fox – This card often represents employment. It covers any job in which a person is employed by others.
- The Bear – This card often represents management or owning a business.
- The Fish – This card represents entrepreneurial endeavors, trading, or jobs in finance.
- The Anchor – This card represents military positions or any sort of training.

The cards listed above can also represent people and can be added to your list of people in the cards. This would mean that the Fox is an employee, the Bear is a manager or business owner, the Fish is an entrepreneur, and the Anchor is someone with a military career.

What would you add to that list? Which cards would you use to describe homemaking, delivery services, or computer services?

Let's try combining these working cards with the Garden. Following are some possibilities that may inspire you. Select other cards to pair the working cards with. Jot down your observations.
- Fox /Garden – Employment in landscaping or working on a crew for events or parties.
- Bear/Garden – Landscaping crew supervisor or business, maybe party organizing.
- Fish/Garden – Custom jobs that are not normally part of landscaping, such as pond installations.
- Anchor/Garden – Job training for a garden center or being stationed at a recruiting station.

Money Cards

How do you look at money? The following two lovely cards are the symbols that typically represent money in

the deck. They speak for themselves as they have both been identified with money through the centuries.
- Clover – Luck/Opportunities
- Fish – Increase

Which one speaks to you as hard cold cash? Which one looks lucrative? Which one symbolizes increase? Is there another card you would use in the deck to represent money? If so, and you are clear about its meaning then add it to your list.

Figure 4h

What happens when you pair the Clover or Fish with other cards? For example, say you have the Clover with the Letter (Figure 4h). What could that represent?

Intimate Relationships in the Cards

This is a nontraditional description list that I use to enhance my readings. I use suggestions like these when I know I'm doing a reading involving a relationship. Feel free to use it, develop it, or discard it.

- The Snake – The other woman or a person that is very difficult such as a stalker.
- The Bouquet – Romance.
- The Whip – Hot passion built on crazy infatuation that, after a few months, may burn out and become tense rather than intense.
- The Child – Childish behavior, immaturity, young love, nostalgia.
- The Stork – A new relationship, new beginning, or someone expecting.
- The Dog – A friendly relationship. This could include friends with benefits, open relationships, a friend or querent that desires more, or a loyal partner.
- The Heart – True sincere love.
- The Ring – The committed partner or the commitment itself.
- The Letter – Love letter or note.
- The Gentleman – A person in the relationship.

- The Lady – A person in the relationship.
- The Lilies – Mature and experienced love or passion.

Practice using the relationship cards in 2 Card Combinations by placing each of them, one at a time, in position 1. Then, lay out the remaining cards one by one in position 2. How does it change the meanings of the cards listed above?

Opposing Cards

Opposing cards don't really exist in the deck, but some of the cards may seem like they don't combine well together. For instance, the Sun and the Moon may seem conflicting. Literally, this reading may be difficult to understand. In a case like this, if you feel a little stuck, get out your PAMs or Keywords list and read the cards according to their position.

Another pairing that will sometimes confuse people is the Gentleman and Lady cards together. This may be a couple or connection of some kind. You may want to experiment with how you will read them together. All that being said, if you use the position 1/position 2 method it will create an easy reading.

Posing Questions

An open reading is a reading in which the cards are pulled without a specific question in mind. By doing this, the subject matter is sought out within the reading. So, within a 2 Card Combination, the subject will be the card in position 1.

Most small or medium-sized readings, however, will be pulled with the intent of answering a question. Often times questions are vague or may be answered with simple yes/no responses. Therefore, it is helpful to elaborate, be specific, and leave the question open-ended. If possible, pose the question in a positive way, stay focused on yourself/the querent, and avoid questions using the word "should." Though, in any reading, a general statement may be made like "I would like to know more about my relationship with my partner" or "I would like insight into why I self-sabotage my projects." If reading for yourself, following are some lead-ins that may be helpful:

- How can I...
- How might I...
- How would I...
- What do I ...
- What is/are...
- What might I...

Yes/No Answers

The cards may be used to receive yes/no answers. Do not read the cards themselves, simply examine them. Following are three methods:
- Draw one card and use the card designation of black or red. A black correspondence symbol on the card indicates a "yes" while a red correspondence symbol indicates a "no." For instance, a black club would be a yes card while a red heart card will be a no card.
- Draw one card and use the card's attribute of positive, negative, and neutral as yes, no and maybe.
- Draw three cards and use the cards' attributes and determine how many positive, negative, or neutral cards you have pulled. For instance, if you have

pulled two negative cards and a positive card, this may mean "probably not." This will work best if you have previously assigned an equal amount of attributes to the cards in the deck (twelve of each).

Homework:

First, practice 2 Card Combinations extensively. Use the whole deck by laying out two cards at a time, make an evaluation of the pair, and repeat the process by laying out cards on top of the previous two cards. When you are done with the deck, you'll end up with two stacks of eighteen cards. Then, switch the piles (making the first cards the second cards) and evaluate the combinations one at a time. Your assessments should be different because the main subject of each combination has changed. Try sharing the experience with friends; it's a fun little game.

Second, if you want to make a more thorough list for pairings, get out your Lenormand notebook and write a Combinations List for each card.

After that, describe a person. Start with your Significator cards (the Lady and the Gentleman). Lay out the Gentleman or Lady card in position 1. Shuffle the rest of the deck and add a card to position 2. How do you describe that person? Lay down the next card on the top of your card in position 2. Now, how do you describe that person? Continue adding cards to the pile of cards in position 2 until you have used the remaining cards in the deck. Each time you put a new card in position 2, describe the person in a new way.

Next, pull the work cards from the deck and shuffle the rest. Lay out a second card next to each one of the work cards. Describe the career you see in each combination.

Then, practice posing questions.
Finally, practice answering yes/no questions. Try using both the card designation of black or red and the card attributes of positive, negative, and neutral.

Chapter 5: Step 3: Card Lines

Step 3: Card Lines

At this point, you should have a very clear understanding of the 2 Card Combination and the relevance of the positions in it. It's time to expand your understanding and create some visual stories through the use of card lines.

3 Card Line

The 3 Card Line is the most commonly used grouping for quick and efficient readings. However, that third card often causes confusion in interpretation if it is not clarified and understood.

The third card position in the following Methods 1 and 2 are unique because the third card is used exclusively for 3 Card Lines; we will not be using the third card position in Methods 1 and 2 in larger Lenormand spreads. Instead, Methods 3 and 4 will become the methods in which we build upon in later steps.

Method 1: Sentence Structure Pieces

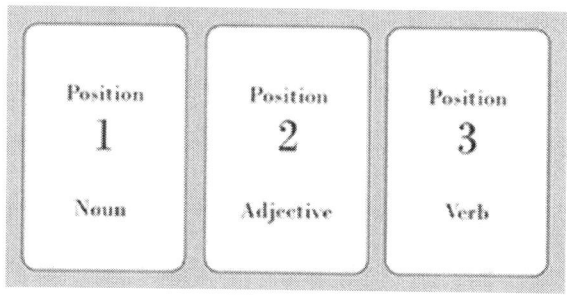

Figure 5a

The most commonly used method for 3 Card Combinations is a sentence structure, though this method was developed in Europe and is not formatted as English sentence structure. The way that actual sentences fit together won't match the card positions of 1, 2 or 3. However, if we pick apart the sentence and then use its pieces, the method works well.

Shuffle and pull 3 cards for Method 1 (Figure 5a). The card in position 1 will be a noun from your PAMs or Suggested Keyword list. The card in position 2 is an adjective, so again select a keyword. The final card in this method is a verb, so select another keyword that makes sense for the card you pulled.

To complicate matters, some people prefer to use this third card as the "period" or "object" of a sentence. If that interests you, I suggest you return to this method after you are comfortable with the cards to explore this option more thoroughly.

Figure 5b

As an example, we will use the above cards (Figure 5b) to describe a material item. We could use the Ship as a "car/vehicle," the Lilies as "classic," and the Rider as "speeding."

Method 2: Subject, Adjective, Cause

This method is a modification of Method 1. The layout and concept are similar to Method 1, but it is read differently.

Pull three cards and lay them in their positions. The card in position 1 will be the subject or topic of the reading. The card in position 2 will be an adjective to the card in position 1; this card adds details to the first by describing it. The final card, in position 3, may represent the reason behind the given situation - the "how" or "cause" of it - in the first two cards. If you elect to use this reading method for your 3 Card Line, be sure to be clear about how you will read position 3 and how *it connects to the first two positions*.

I've observed many variations of how people use this 3 Card Line in this way. I use this method often when I want a quick answer.

Method 3: Pair Chain

This method will later be used in larger spreads. For the most part, you know how to read the cards in this way because you already know how to read 2 Card Combinations, the difference is that other 2 Card Combinations are added on to the previous pairing.

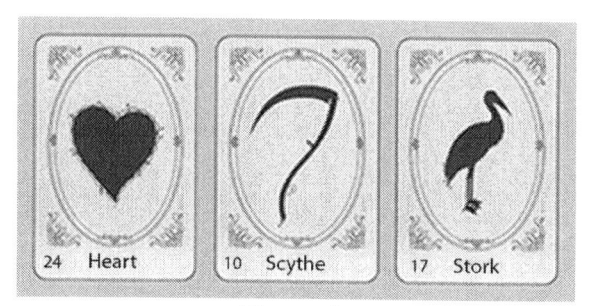

Figure 5c

If the Heart, the Scythe, and the Stork are pulled (Figure 5c), the combination would be broken down into 2 pairs: Heart and Scythe plus Scythe and Stork. However, they are part of the same set, so they need to be looked at in a cohesive way to see the entire picture. Breaking the combinations apart, I may say the Heart and Scythe are a broken heart and that the Scythe and Stork might be a fresh ending. Looking at the cards cohesively, I may derive that someone has had their heart broken, but that it will create a fresh beginning.

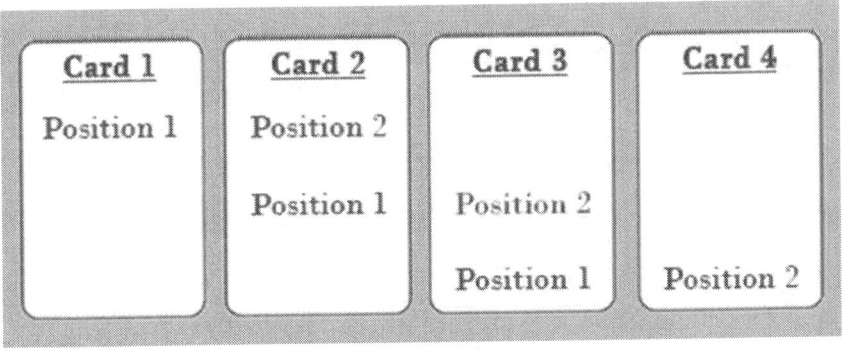

Figure 5d

Later, when using longer lines of cards in readings, the progression continues. In the sequence of four cards (Figure 5d), position 1 and position 2 are the same as the positions in the 2 Card Combination. Then the card in position 2 becomes its own position 1 and the third card becomes position 2 in this combination. Each additional card pairing (2 Card Combination) adds to the information of the prior card combinations.

Method 4: Flanking Description Cards

The following method is distinctly different from the above methods because the cards are not read from right to left. Like Method 3, this method will be used later in larger spreads.

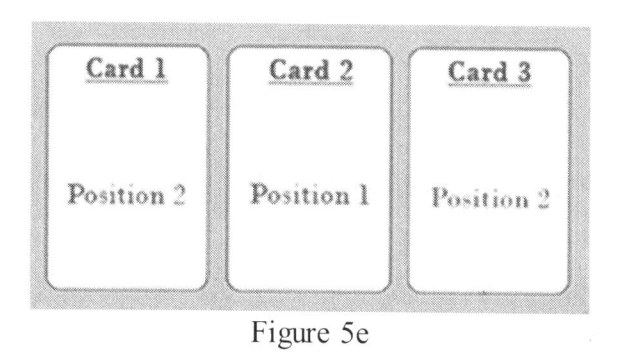

Card 1	Card 2	Card 3
Position 2	Position 1	Position 2

Figure 5e

After shuffling, the cards may be laid out in one of two ways.
 1) In consecutive order.
 2) Put down the center card first, then the cards on the left and right.

Regardless of the order the cards are laid out, the center card becomes the subject and the flanking cards on either side both add a description to the center card. It is read similar to two 2 Card Combinations, only now being read in two directions and with one subject card.

Card Clusters

When using multiple sets of 3 Card Lines, I call these "clusters." It is a convenient way to read multiple outcomes or to modify existing spread layouts.

For instance, if a querent is inquiring about work and has multiple job options it would be beneficial to pull a 3 Card Line for each option to see which option is the most promising or beneficial. Or, let's say a querent wants to move and they are considering three different areas they might want to relocate. By using 3 Card Lines to predict the likely experience of each area, the querent may gain a better understanding of what to expect from each location, therefore narrowing their search.

Clusters can also be used to predict future events. For instance, let's pretend you have ordered a new custom car that is guaranteed to come in within the next four weeks. Lay out four 3 Card Lines to determine which week is likely to be the week it will arrive.

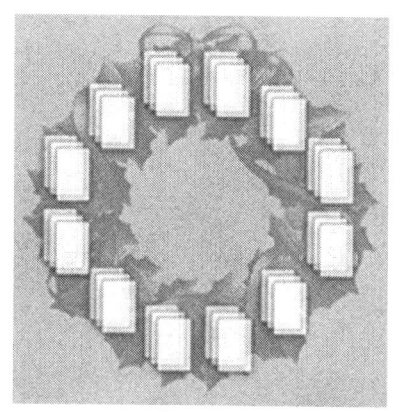

Figure 5f

Try doing a yearly reading to forecast events of the upcoming months. In the above circular spread, the 3 Card Lines are read for the twelve months of the year (Figure 5f). I do this reading every January 1st!

Figure 5g

The spread in Figure 5g is also a yearly reading in which each 3 Card Line represents a month. It separates the quarters of a year by using four rows of three sets/clusters of 3 Card Lines (this can also be done with the seasons of a year). The first row represents the first-quarter of the year (January, February, and March). The second row represents the second-quarter of the year (April, May, and June). The third row represents the third-quarter of the year (July, August, and September). The fourth row represents the fourth-quarter of the year (October, November, December).

As stated previously, Lenormand and Tarot *cards* are not compatible reading systems and cannot be interchanged. However, the spread layouts from each system can be used. 3 Card Lines may be used in lieu of individual Tarot cards in any one Tarot position. The Tarot spreads can only have twelve positions or less because of the number of cards available in a Lenormand deck. However, custom spreads don't need to be Tarot spreads.

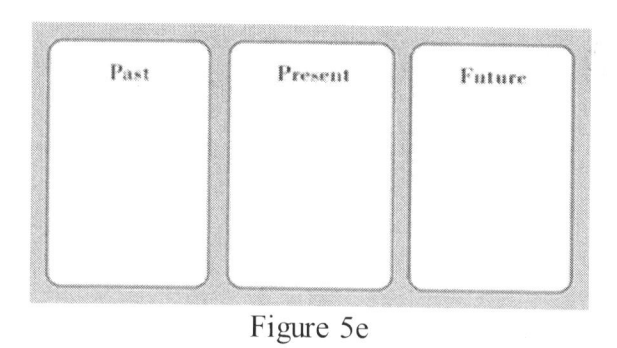

Figure 5e

A very common Tarot spread is Past-Present-Future (Figure 5e). In this spread, place a 3 Card Line in each position (for a total of nine cards).

The following information is for Tarot practitioners; skip this paragraph if you aren't familiar with Tarot terminology. Try using the Celtic Cross Spread with 3 Card Lines in each of the spread's positions. I commonly use an Elements spread which uses the four Tarot suits. Consider the suits and what each of them represents; pull the aces from a Tarot deck if that helps. By laying 3 Card Lines in each area (ultimately using twelve cards total) a well-rounded reading develops.

5 Card Line

Here are three ways in which you can pull and place your 5 Card Line. The positions will be in order from 1 to 5.
1. The first and most common way is to shuffle the deck and then simply put down five cards in consecutive order off the top of the deck.
2. The second way is to pull a focus card (a card that represents what the querent's question is about) from the deck and then place it in position 3. After that, shuffle and place the other cards around it (positions 1 and 2, then positions 4 and 5).
3. The third way is to predetermine your focus card. Then, shuffle with all the cards in the deck including the focus card and keep the deck in your hands (without pulling any cards). Flip the deck over and look for the focus card. Once the focus card is located, pull it and two cards on either side

of it from the deck and lay them out in the order you found them in. If the focus card is near the end of the deck, preventing you from being able to pull a full five cards, repeat the process until you have all five cards to pull.

| 14 Fox | 2 Clover | 34 Fish | 19 Tower | 15 Bear |

Figure 5h

You already know how to read the cards in positions 3, 4, and 5 (Figure 5h). How so? Simply by laying the positions of the 3 Card Line: Method 3 over the last three cards of the 5 Card Line (in this case the cards would be the Fish, the Tower, and the Bear). In other words, the 3 Card Line: Method 3 fills-in positions 3, 4, and 5 of the 5 Card Line. Confused? Look at the five cards you have already pulled. Flip the first two cards so they are face down and leave the remaining three cards face up. The three cards on the right are read just like the 3 Card Line: Method 3. To clarify, continue using Figure 5i and 5j.

Figure 5i

In Figure 5i, we see a face-down card, another face-down card, the Heart, the Scythe, and the Stork. By flipping the first two cards over in the 5 Card Line, the remaining three cards are read as a 3 Card Line: Method 3.

Figure 5j

Now, turn over the first two cards in positions 1 and 2 (Figure 5j). The center three cards are read just as the 3 Card Line: Method 4, the only difference being that the combinations are extended outward. Work your way out from the center of the five cards. Even though position 1 in this reading is technically the first card on the left, it will not be the starting point of this reading.

This is because the card in position 1 describes the card in position 2. The card in position 2 describes the card in position 3. The card in position 4 also describes the card in position 3. The card in position 5 describes the card in position 4.

The 5 Card Line contains a past, present, and future timeline. Ignore the cards in position 1 and position 2 for the moment and evaluate the cards moving to the right in positions 3, 4, and 5. The combination of the cards in positions 3 and 4 represent what is presently happening. The combination of the cards in positions 4 and 5 represent the direction the future is going. Now, we go the other direction and move from the center to the left. The combination of the cards in positions 3 and 2 represent a transition from the past to what is currently happening. The combination of the cards in positions 2 and 1 represent the past.

This spread may be read with a Significator or preselected focus card in the center position. Let's say you have placed the Gentleman in the center of the reading. Now, imagine he is a real person that is facing you. He stretches his arms out to indicate his past and future; His right arm will be the past, his left arm will be the future, and he is in the center of his story.

Another way to imagine how time is read in the 5 Card Line is to compare it to an open book. Imagine a book lays open with its spine down and pages up. About half of the pages are on the left and half of the pages are on the right. You would have already read the pages on the left. The pages that are open are where you are currently reading. The pages on the right are what are left to read.

Sometimes when the cards are pulled, those cards will describe a future you already know is coming. In this case, it may be helpful to add additional future cards to the right of the reading. Do not change the positions of the original 5 Card Line you laid down, the first two positions will remain the past. Each card that is added on to the right side of the reading will create another pair in the chain and a progression in time. The periods of time may be set to specific increments (days, weeks, or months). This is a very convenient way to be able to discern timing in card lines.

Bookends
Bookends are used exclusively in 5 Card Lines. Pair only the cards in position 1 and position 5, temporarily ignoring the cards in between. Read the bookends as a 2 Card Combination (card 1 becomes position 1 and

card 5 becomes position 2 of the combination). If we use Figure 5j the Bookends would be the Tree and the Stork. This pairing would describe the theme of the reading.

Lenormand and Tarot
Side by Side Readings

It is amazing what can be gleaned by reading Lenormand and Tarot side by side. If you use Tarot, try using a Tarot Past-Present-Future next to a Lenormand 5 Card Line. Usually, the 2 different systems will deliver similar messages.

Homework:

Explore the 3 Methods of the 3 Card Line. Decide which you are most comfortable with. Make sure that you understand Methods 3 and 4 because they will be used in larger spreads.

Then, lay out 3 Card Lines, one on top of the other, for practice. First, lay down three cards and interpret them. Then, right on top of the existing set, lay down another set. Once you have interpreted that set, lay down another set, etc. This is also enjoyable as a game with friends or at a party. It is a quick way to show others how to use the cards and it is fun to see their reactions. Use 3 Card Lines in clusters, such as a yearly reading or a Tarot spread.

Once comfortable with 3 Card Lines, move on to 5 Card Lines. If you like, add additional cards to the right for an extended look into the future.

If you use Tarot, try using 3 Card Lines in Tarot spread positions. Also, do a side-by-side Lenormand and Tarot reading using a Lenormand 5 Card Line and a three Tarot card spread.

Remember to write your card lines, spreads, interpretations, and conclusions in your notebook.

Chapter 6: Step 4: 9 Card Square

Step 4: The 9 Card Square

Figure 6a

The 9 Card Square, also known as the 3x3 or Square of Nine, is a medium-sized spread that is commonly used.

It provides a more comprehensive reading than card lines but is less daunting than the complex tableaus.

In addition, the 9 Card Square can serve as a precursor for larger spreads. Like the smaller readings we have used, it is built upon the lessons you have already learned. And, once this spread is understood, it creates a foundation for using the Grand Tableau.

There are a few different ways to lay the cards out in the 9 Card Square:
1. The first and most common way is to shuffle and then place the cards in consecutive order by row - the first three cards in the first row, the second three cards in the second row, and the third three cards in the third row.
2. The second way is to preselect a focus card from the deck and place it in the center position. After that, shuffle and place the other cards around it in consecutive order – the first row, cards 4 and 6 of the second row, then the third row.
3. Use a pattern that incorporates the corners or the cross within the spread.

The 9 Card Square Format

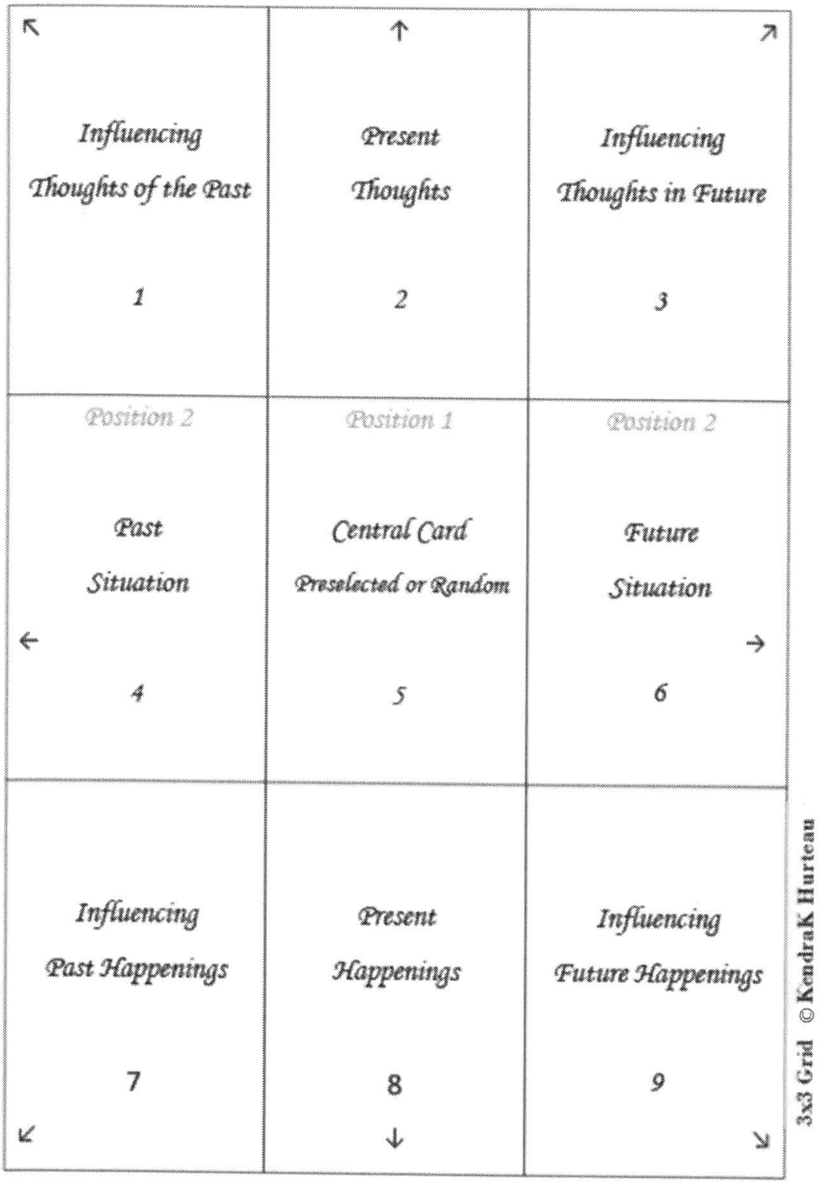

| Influencing Thoughts of the Past

1 | Present Thoughts

2 | Influencing Thoughts in Future

3 |
|---|---|---|
| *Position 2*

Past Situation

4 | *Position 1*

Central Card Preselected or Random

5 | *Position 2*

Future Situation

6 |
| Influencing Past Happenings

7 | Present Happenings

8 | Influencing Future Happenings

9 |

Figure 6b

3x3 Grid © Kendra K Hurteau

- 81 -

Like with the 5 Card Line, the cards of the 9 Card Square are read outward from the central card position (Figure 6b). The central card is the focus of the reading and acts as the first card in the 2 Card Combinations used within the spread. The card in position 6 acts as the second card in a 2 Card Combination. And, actually, each of the surrounding cards to the central card also acts as a second card of a 2 Card Combination, though their placement makes the meaning of that combination different than the others. Because it is a natural inclination to read the cards from right to left, this is often times where people get confused. However, in a 9 Card Square, the only pair read in a left to right line is the cards in positions 5 and 6. The rest of the pairings are read outward from the central card (5+1, 5+2, 5+3, 5+4, 5+7, 5+8, 5+9).

Note: There is a larger copy of the 3x3 Grid in the Appendix.

The cards are read in a cohesive way with each card affected by another card, though each position has its own unique function. A situation is represented, timing is determined, thoughts and beliefs are revealed, and reality is addressed. To further distinguish each card position in the 9 Card Square, a breakdown follows.

Rows

The rows of a 9 Card Square distinguish different parts of the querent's life experience. The top row (positions 1, 2 and 3) represents the thoughts or beliefs of the querent. The center row (positions 4, 5, and 6) is the situation unfolding or being addressed. I like to look at the row as the perspective of the querent. The bottom row (positions 7, 8 and 9) represents things that are happening in the querent's reality. As a reminder, cards are combined as 2 Card Combinations.

- Situation. Because the cards are read outward from the central card, start by reading the second row. The second row is read as two 2 Card Combinations (5+4 and 5+6).
- Thoughts. The cards in the first row are first read in relationship to the central card, acting as they would as cards in the second position of a 2 Card Combination (5+1, 5+2, and 5+3). Then, to understand more about the thoughts of the querent, the cards may be read in connection with the other cards in that same row. They are read outward from position 2 (2+1 and 2+3).
- Reality. The same method will be used in the third row as in the first row. The cards in the third column are read in relationship to the central card,

acting as they would as cards in the second position of a 2 Card Combination (5+7, 5+8, and 5+9). Then, to understand more about the life of the querent, the cards may be read in connection with the other cards in the same row. They are read outward from position 8 (8+7 and 8+9).

Columns

The columns of the 9 Card Square distinguish generalized time periods. The first column (positions 1, 4, and 7) represents the past, the second column (positions 2, 5, and 8) represents the present, and the third column (positions 3, 6, and 9) represents the future.

- Present. Because the cards are read outward from the central card, start with reading the second column. The second column is read as two combinations (5+2 and 5+8).
- Past. The cards in the first column are read in relationship to the central card, acting as they would as cards in the second position of a 2 Card Combination (5+1, 5+4, and 5+7). To get a clearer picture of the past, the cards may then be read in connection with the other cards in the

same column and will be read outward from position 4 (4+1 and 4+7).
- Future. The same method will be used in the third column as in the first column. The cards in the third column are read in relationship to the central card, acting as they would as cards in the second position of a 2 Card Combination (5+3, 5+6, and 5+9). To glean a better understanding of what will be happening in the future, the cards may then read in connection with the other cards in the same column and are read outward from position 6 (6+3 and 6+9).

Diagonal Lines

The cards in the diagonal lines of a 9 Card Square (positions 1, 5, and 9 plus positions 7, 5, and 3) distinguish influencing situations. In any given issue there are always outside influences or circumstances. As with reading the rows and columns, these cards are read outward from the center. The cards running from the top left to the bottom right will be read as 2 Card Combinations (5+1 and 5+9). Then, the cards running from the bottom left to the top right will be read in the same way (5+7 and 5+3).

Specific Cards

If you want to know more about a specific card that interests you, it is possible to read from that position. For example, if you selected the card in position 7, then you would read the cards to the right of it because there are no cards to the left (7+8+9). If you selected the card in position 8, then you would read outward from the center to the left and right (8+7 and 8+9). If you selected the card in position 9, then you would read the cards to the left of it (9+8+7).

Diamond

Reading the cards that shape a diamond (positions 2, 6, 8, 4, and 2) within the 9 Card Square is also an option. Read the cards in a pair chain (2+6, 6+8, 8+4, 4+2) just as in the 3 Card Line: Method 3 (Figure 5d).

The 9 Card Square Quick Reference Guide

Initially, the intricacies of the 9 Card Square may seem daunting. I assure you that it will become very comprehensible with a little practice. Let's summarize a 9 Card Square reading for clarification.
1) Decide your question or choose the situation you want to read about, be clear about how you will use the cards, and then shuffle the deck.
2) Lay the cards out in consecutive order or pull a focus card first and then place cards in the remaining positions.
3) The central card is the main subject. That card is affected by all of the other cards around it. So, it is paired with the surrounding cards.
   a) Evaluate the cards in each row.
      i) Row 1 (1, 2, and 3) shows what the querent is thinking.
      ii) Row 2 (4, 5, and 6) shows the situation as it is unfolding.
      iii) Row 3 (7, 8, and 9) shows events or things happening in the life of the querent.
   b) Look at the cards in each column for the timeline.

      i) Column 1 (cards 1, 4, and 7) represents the past.
     ii) Column 2 (cards 2, 5, and 8) represents the present.
    iii) Column 3 (cards 3, 6, and 9) represents the future.

4) Look at the diagonal lines to better understand influencing circumstances.
    a) Cards 1, 5, and 9
    b) Cards 7, 5, and 3

5) Once all the combinations are evaluated, an overall assessment usually comes naturally. If not, take a few moments to contemplate what the reading is saying as a whole.

11 Card Spread

Figure 6c

By adding two cards to either side of the second row of a 9 Card Square (the Tree and the Whip), you can create an 11 Card Spread. This spread may also aid in your step by step progress to reading larger spreads. Remember that the card combinations are first read outward from the central card (the Moon in this case).

Place the cards just as you would a 9 Card Square, but include five cards in the second row. This means that the first row contains positions 1 thru 3, the second row contains positions 4 thru 8, and the third row contains positions 9 thru 11.

This 11 Card Spread contains both the 5 Card Line and the 9 Card Square (Figure 6c). It is essentially read the same way as a 9 Card Square, with the addition of extra cards in the second row that extend the timeline. Plus, the bookends of the 5 Card Line establish a theme.

The layout contains the following card spreads discussed so far.
- 2 Card Combination
- 3 Card Line: Method 3
- 3 Card Line: Method 4
- 5 Card Line
- 9 Card Square

Other Medium-Sized Spreads

Though our focus is on the development of the Grand Tableau, the following additional medium-sized spreads may interest you.

Figure 6d

The Cross Spread (Figure 6d) has various uses. Most commonly it is considered an expansion of the 3 Card Line: Method 4 or a shortened version of the 9 Card Square. By omitting the corners, influencing lines and details in the timeline are missing.

Figure 6e

The 8 Card Spread (Figure 6e) may be used for an either/or answer. Read the two separate rows as pair chains (3 Card Combination: Method 3, Figure 5d) to identify two different answers. Example questions follow: Should I move to California or Nevada? Should I join the swimming team or the baseball team? Should I buy the red car or the white car?

Figure 6f

The Pyramid Spread (Figure 6f), is a little unconventional. Preselect a focus card for the top of the spread before shuffling cards for the rest of the spread. There are two ways to read this spread.
1. The focus card won't really be "read" because it stands alone. The second row will represent current situations and be read as a 2 Card Combination. The third row will represent an underlying circumstance and be read as a 3 Card Line: Method 3 or 4.
2. The top card will act as the first card in a 2 Card Combination and the cards in the second row will

- 93 -

act as second cards in that combination. In this way, the focus card can now be read. That means that the top three cards will be read as a subject card with two descriptor cards. Next, as a second part of the reading, the two cards in the second row describe an underlying situation. They become the subject cards for which the cards in the third row describe them. The bottom five cards should be read as two subject cards with the remaining three cards as descriptor cards. These combinations function with the intent of a 2 Card Combination, except that the layout is different.

Homework:

Read several 9 Card Squares. Once you are comfortable with the layout, read for others if possible.

Try out other medium-sized spreads.

Write your spreads, interpretations, and conclusions in your notebook.

Chapter 7: Step 5: Petit Tableau

Step 5: The Petit Tableau

Figure 7a

The Petit Tableau, originally titled the "Mini Tableau," is a spread I designed. I first shared it on YouTube and then published it in the little white book for the Under the Roses Lenormand deck. At the time I designed the Petit Tableau, I was looking for a spread that was larger than the 9 Card Spread and smaller than the Grand Tableau.

The French word "tableau" means arrangement (see Terminology). In the French language, the word "petit" means small and the word "grand" means great or large. Therefore, the Petit Tableau is a small arrangement of images and the Grand Tableau (covered in the next chapter) is a large arrangement of images.

The Petit Tableau is a thorough reading and is another step in undertaking the large spreads.

The Petit Tableau Format

The Petit Tableau is laid out with three rows of five cards and a fourth row of three cards. It is a great fifteen to thirty-minute reading. Like other spreads, you may select a subject or Significator for the center of the second row before shuffling.

We are going to use the techniques from previous chapters to make sense of the Petit Tableau. Remember how 2 Card Combinations fit well into the 9 Card Square? Now, we will use the 9 Card Square to aid in understanding this more elaborate spread (Figure 7a).

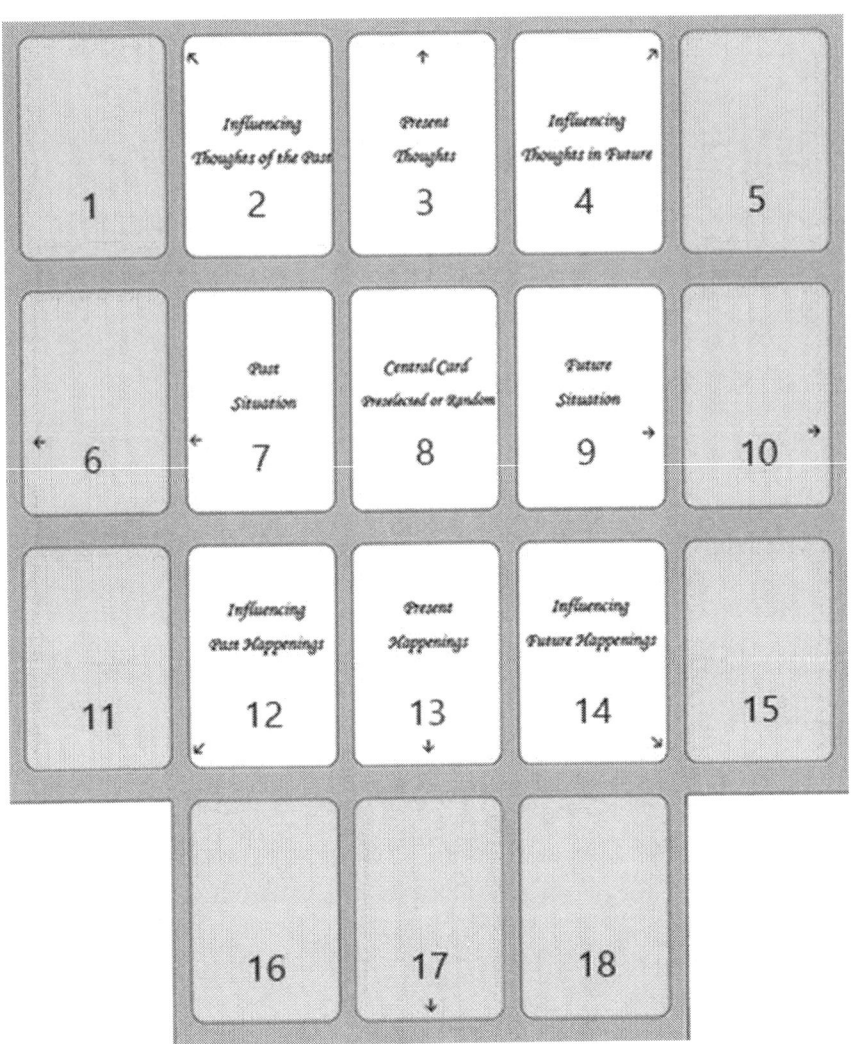

1	*Influencing Thoughts of the Past* 2	*Present Thoughts* 3	*Influencing Thoughts in Future* 4	5
6	*Past Situation* 7	*Central Card Preselected or Random* 8	*Future Situation* 9	10
11	*Influencing Past Happenings* 12	*Present Happenings* 13	*Influencing Future Happenings* 14	15
	16	17	18	

Figure 7b

Shuffle, pull, and place cards according to the diagram in Figure 7b. Should you turn the first column, the last column, and the bottom row facedown then a familiar pattern appears. In the center is a 9 Card Square, which you already know how to read. Now, flip all the cards

- 98 -

face up and continue reading outward from the central card (position 8) extending the reading lines.

You will also find that the 5 Card Line is in the second row because of the placement of the central card. Though you already know how to read the 5 Card Line, it is necessary to omit the use of the bookends technique because the theme of the reading will now be established a different way.

Theme Corners

The four corners, which are also referred to as "cornerstones," of the spread represent a theme for the reading. Interpret these two combinations to establish the theme:

- The top left and bottom right positions (1+15)
- The bottom left and top right positions (11+5)

Destiny Cards

The row at the bottom of the Petit Tableau contains "destiny cards" or "fate cards." These cards provide a more profound look into the future of one's life as a whole. Sometimes we get stuck on what's happening to us right now and forget that our entire life contains lessons or experiences that aren't limited to our current circumstances. The destiny cards provide an opportunity to look deeper into the querent's overall life experience. Use card 17 as the subject and use the flanking cards on either side to add descriptions to it (3 Card Line: Method 4).

Timeline

Evaluating timing within spreads can be tricky unless it is clearly defined before laying out the cards. Lenormand can help specify the time by designating the columns as weeks or months in any spread that contains past, present, and future positions. As a result, the generalized timeline of the 5 Card Line or 9 Card Square (Past-Present-Future) can then be defined. It is also possible to declare your intention that the timeline will be a month, five weeks, or six weeks to the Petit Tableau. This makes it very handy to use the Petit Tableau as a monthly reading.

Petit Tableau with Houses

As an additional option, there is an advanced technique called "houses." It is best if you are already comfortable with the Petit Tableau before adding this technique to the spread.

Houses work well with this eighteen card spread because the entire thirty-six card deck will be used in the layout. It is best if a focus card is not pulled in advance when using this technique.

Figure 7c

- 101 -

As you know by now, Lenormand cards are usually read in pairs. However, here is an exception to that rule. Each "house" represents an aspect or area of the querent's life. The house cards are placed in the initial eighteen positions and will provide more background information for the cards that are placed on top. They are placeholders or groundwork, an extra bottom layer of cards (Figure 7c), for the reading to come. The houses will not be read as combinations and are incomplete without the reading cards on top of them. Some people look at these cards as another descriptor card to the card that is on top of it, but the cards aren't intended to be used that way. If anything, the top cards would be a descriptor card to the house card.

Remember, the houses are talking about aspects of life. If the fish house is underneath, this would likely be about the querent's financial life. If the tree house is underneath, this would likely be about the querent's health. The fox house might represent career, the dog house might represent friendships, or the garden house might represent a community. For instance, if you have the Mountain on top of the ring house this will likely be about a blockage in the querent's commitments. If a querent wants to know what is going on in their finances and there is a fish house, look at the card which falls in that fish house. Similarly, if a querent wants to know more about what is happening in their career and there is a fox house, look to see which card falls in that fox house.

Though house meanings are not necessarily based on keywords, you will likely have a good inclination to what each house might represent from your existing list of keywords. It may be beneficial to make an extra list of house meanings. A sample list follows.

Sample House Meanings

- Rider – Things upcoming
- Clover – Fortune, as in fortunate or unfortunate
- Ship – Travel
- House – Family or household
- Tree – Health
- Clouds – Things unforeseen
- Snake – Things to look out for
- Coffin – Big transitions and loss
- Bouquet – Gifts and Abundance
- Scythe – Things ending
- Whip – Things repeating
- Birds – Communication
- Child – Recreation
- Fox – Career
- Bear – Parents
- Stars – Possibilities
- Stork – New beginnings
- Dog – Friendship
- Tower – Changing perspectives
- Garden – Community
- Mountain – Hard challenges
- Crossroads – Pressing decisions
- Mice – Mounting problems

- Heart – Love life
- Ring – Commitment
- Book – Education
- Letter – Results
- Gentleman – The querent or a significant person
- Lady – The querent or a significant person
- Lilies – Well-being
- Sun – Success
- Moon – Emotions
- Key – Forthcoming answers
- Fish – Finance
- Anchor – Stability
- Cross – Spirituality or burdens

The Petit Tableau Quick Reference Guide

1) Shuffle the deck with clear intentions.
2) If using houses, the house cards are placed in their eighteen house positions. Do not read the house cards together as a reading. They are simply placeholders for the reading that will be laid on top of them.
3) Lay out the eighteen cards that you will read with in their positions as shown in Figure 7b (on top of the previous house cards if applicable, Figure 7c). If you elect to use a focus card, pull it from the deck and place it in the central card position (position 8) beforehand.
4) Read the (top) cards outwards from the central card position (position 8), by following the horizontal, vertical and diagonal lines.
5) Notice the timeline as you read the combinations and lines.
6) Read the cornerstones.
7) Read the destiny cards.
8) To find out which house any particular top card is in, simply lift the top card to find out which house is underneath.

Homework:

Read several Petit Tableaus and plan on spending twenty to thirty minutes with each one. Eventually, you'll gain speed and the readings will take ten to twenty minutes apiece. Take time getting to know the Petit Tableau because it will save time later when we take on the Grand Tableau. Plus, the Petit Tableau is a great all-around spread that you may end up using consistently. It provides detail and can be done in a relatively short amount of time.

Write your spreads, interpretations, and conclusions in your notebook.

Write a House Meanings list in which you describe each area/aspect of life the cards represent.

Practice the Petit Tableau with houses.

Chapter 8: Step 6: Grand Tableau

Step 6: The Grand Tableaus

You have done it! You have made it to the Grand Tableau lesson. Don't let the size of this spread intimidate you. Because we have been going step by step, you already have the necessary skills to tackle these large spreads. You will now apply what you know and add more intricacies to the reading.

The Grand Tableaus are often affectionately called by their acronym, "GT." There are two different layouts for this spread.

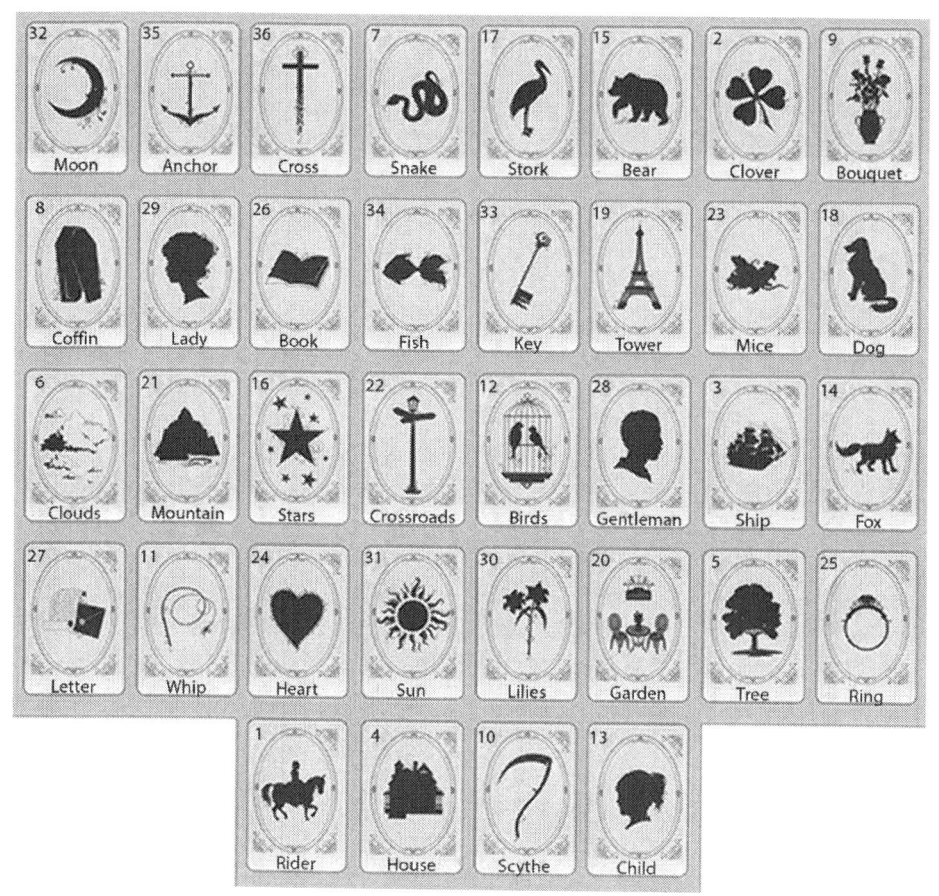

Figure 8a

The first layout style for the Grand Tableau is an 8x4+4 (Figure 8a). The position numbers are laid out as:
01·02·03·04·05·06·07·08
09·10·11·12·13·14·15·16
17·18·19·20·21·22·23·24
25·26·27·28·29·30·31·32
33·34·35·36

- 109 -

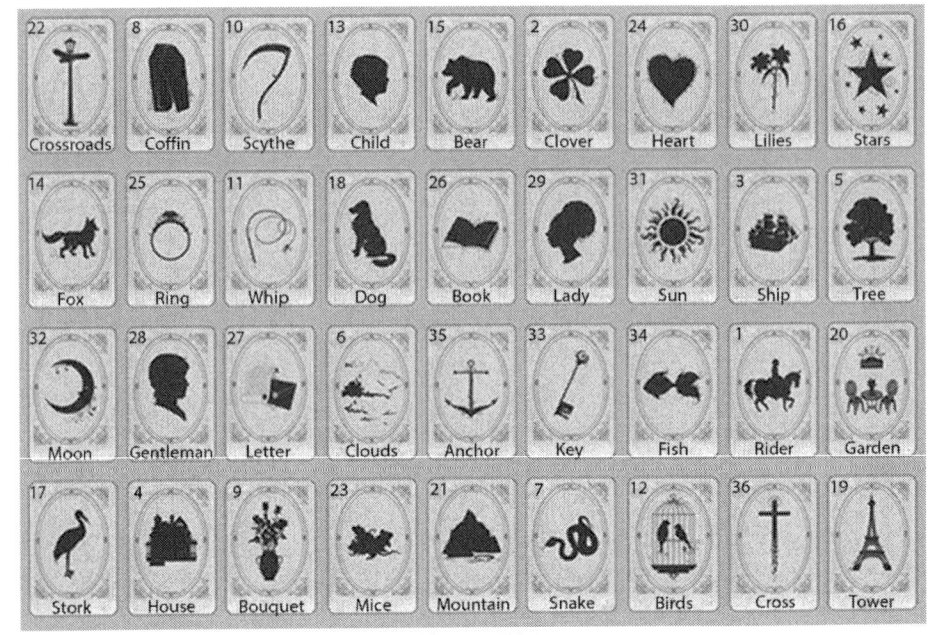

Figure 8b

The second layout style is a 9x4 (Figure 8b). The position numbers are laid out as:

01·02·03·04·05·06·07·08·09
10·11·12·13·14·15·16·17·18
19·20·21·22·23·24·25·26·27
28·29·30·31·32·33·34·35·36

Both versions function similarly and use all thirty-six cards in the deck. The primary difference is that the 8x4+4 is the only one that uses destiny cards.

I look at the Grand Tableau as a "map" or "grid." A map, if you will, will provide locations and roads.

- 110 -

Follow those roads (columns, rows, and diagonal lines) and let them show you where you have been and where you are going. Each time you lay out a new GT it's like looking at a new map. The reading method will be the same, but the destinations are different.

The Grand Tableau is typically read as an open reading, though it is likely the querent may have inquiries in mind beforehand. Naturally, they will also have questions during the reading.

As before, remember to set your intentions and determine your timeline before you shuffle. These simple decisions will prevent second-guessing later. If this isn't done, the reading will likely be muddled. What period of time have you set for the columns? Which techniques will you be using? Then, select one of the layouts, shuffle, and lay out the cards in the spread you have chosen.

The first thing to do is to locate the Significator. If the querent identifies as a woman, then look for the Lady. If the querent identifies as a man, then look for the Gentleman.

If the Significator is in a borderline (the top row, the bottom row, the left column, or the right column), then the information you will get from the spread will be somewhat limited. You may want to reshuffle and lay out a new spread until the Significator falls inside the borderlines. Before you pick up the cards to restart the reading, there is a little bit of information that may help you understand why the Significator originally fell on a borderline.

- The Significator in the top row indicates that the querent is focused on actual things that are happening in their life.
- The Significator in the bottom row indicates that the querent is wrapped up in their thoughts and not in what is currently happening.
- The Significator in the first column indicates the querent is looking to the future and not focused on the past.
- The Significator in the last row indicates that the querent is absorbed in the past and not likely moving on from it; they may recreate the same or similar issues as a result.

If you have a second Lenormand deck, there is another way to deal with this problem. Leave the cards in the order you laid them out (unless the Significator is in a corner, then definitely pick it up). Shuffle a second deck and lay another row or column next to the borderline where the Significator is. In this way, there is a full 3x3 Grid to read around the Significator which is important in the GT.

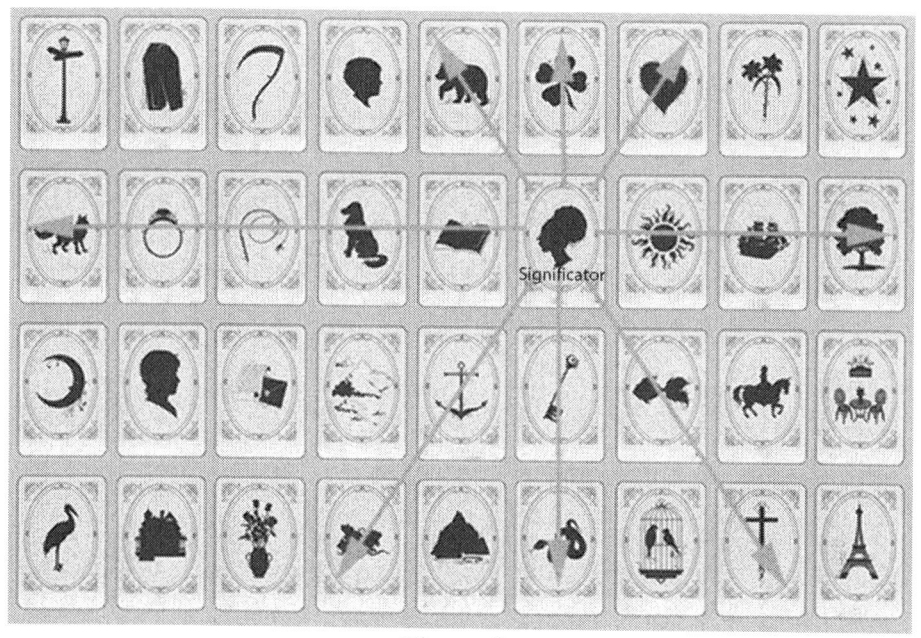

Figure 8c

In all other spreads the central card is stationary. In the Grand Tableau, the Significator is the central card. Here is where that 3x3 Grid is really helpful. Imagine it is printed on transparent paper and that you can lay it on top of the tableau. The Significator will fill the space of the central card box. You already know how to read columns, rows, and diagonals. Now, extend the pair chains out from the Significator (Figure 8c) just as in the 9 Card Square or Petit Tableau.

When following the lines, evaluate the past cards before the future cards. This will confirm that the reading is on track and bring surety and clarity to the interpretation of the future cards.

As previously stated, you are using the time measurement you have selected for each column: weeks, two weeks, or a month. As you do more of these readings you will get more comfortable with how much time to allot to each column. If you are a novice, read the columns as weeks.

There is a variation for how time is used. Some people actually change the direction that time is read according to the direction the Significator faces. That means that if the Significator looks to the left then that is the direction of the future cards. The back of the Significator then faces the past to the right. I don't recommend this approach. It's better to have consistency in the spread, so that every time it is used it functions the same way.

Just like the 9 Card Square, the row the Significator is in represents the situations that are unfolding. Every row above that card will be about the querent's thoughts. Every row below the Significator will represent things happening in the life of the querent. And again, like the 9 Card Square, every column to the left (or behind) the Significator is about the past and every column to their right (or in front) of the Significator is their future.

The horizontal and vertical lines leading away from the Significator create a separation of, what I call, "quadrants." The cards in the space of the upper left quadrant represent past thoughts. The cards in the space of the upper right quadrant represent future thoughts. The cards in the space of the lower left quadrant represent previous events or things that have happened. The cards in the space of the lower right quadrant represent what is going to happen.

Though I do not endorse the following approaches, there are variations of how the rows are used. For instance, the rows above the Significator could represent things that are out of their control and the cards under the Significator would be things in their control. Or, the cards above the Significator could represent the conscious aspects of the querent, while the cards below the Significator would be the subconscious aspects of the querent. If you elect to use a method such as these, make sure that you are clear about what you will do before shuffling the cards.

Grid Shifting
After the Significator is thoroughly explored, it is also possible to explore other subjects by moving the 3x3 Grid over other cards. Say you want to know more about your employment. Find the Fox then follow the lines out from that card. Want to know more about your child? Follow the lines out from the Child. To reiterate, your starting point moves according to the card placement you are reading from, so make sure to start with the Significator and explore other cards after that.

Theme Cards
Many people start their Grand Tableau reading by interpreting the theme before they evaluate the Significator. Yet, this can be done at any point in the reading. There are two ways to read the theme cards in these large readings.
    1) Just as in the Petit Tableau, combine and interpret the two sets of cornerstones and draw a

conclusion about the theme of the reading. In the 8x4+4 GT (Figure 8a) the card combinations are 1+36 and 25+8. In the 9x4 GT (Figure 8b) the card combinations are 1+36 and 28+9.
2) Read the cards that fall in positions 1, 2, and 3 in order as a 3 Card Line.

Destiny Cards of the 8x4+4 GT
Most commonly, I see these cards read from left to right as pair chains. While it is definitely the easier technique, keep in mind that the position of the Significator is relevant. For example, in the 8x4+4 GT (Figure 8a), the Lady is positioned to the left of the destiny cards while the Gentleman is positioned to the right of the cards (though they are not in the same row). If reading the Lady as the Significator, then the above technique would stand true and the cards would be about her future because the cars are on her right. However, if the Gentleman is the Significator, then it doesn't make sense to read the cards from that direction because the cards are on his left. Read the cards in the reverse direction. This would mean that they are about his destiny that has been or is being fulfilled. Should a Significator fall somewhere in the middle of the spread, judge the timeframe in the destiny cards accordingly.

Grand Tableau Advanced Techniques

<u>Houses</u>

Like in the Petit Tableau, the houses represent areas/aspects of life. They lay the groundwork for the cards on top of them. There are two ways to place the houses in the Grand Tableau.

1) The most common method uses the position number to determine the house. If you were to set out all of the cards in order according to the number that is on the card, then those cards would be the positions of the houses. For instance, position 1 will be the Rider because the card is numbered one. The second position will be the Clover because it is numbered two. And in like manner, the thirty-sixth position will be the Cross because that card is numbered 36. Because the house positions are set according to the card number, the spread doesn't require an extra layer of cards. For your convenience, the position numbers are laid out under Figures 8a and 8b.

2) Use two Lenormand decks. Shuffle and layout the first deck with the intention of the cards being used solely as houses. Then, shuffle and lay out the second deck to use as the reading.

There is a chance, with either method, that you will come across two of the same cards in one position; one as the reading card and the other as the house. This is not a problem because they both have separate functions. So, if the Heart is on top of the heart house, then the reading card is about being in love (or whatever your keywords suggest) and its meaning is altered by the top cards around it. The card in the house would be about the querent's love life and is not altered by description. If you get confused, refer to your keywords list or house meanings list for clarification.

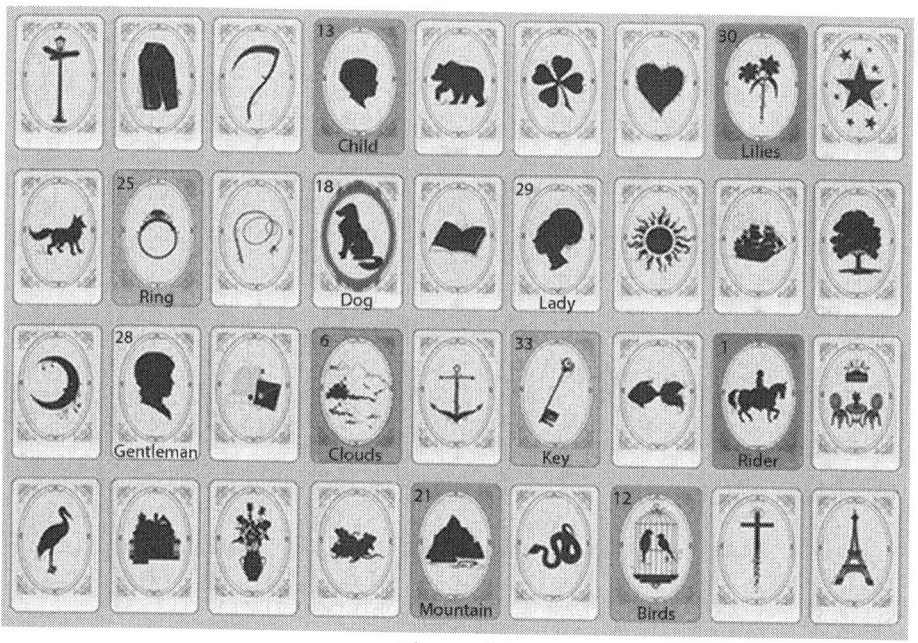

Figure 8d

Mirroring

The mirroring card reveals how the querent appears to others.

The mirroring card is always in the same row with the Significator. Both the Significator and mirroring card positions have the same count outward from the midline of the spread. If you were to fold the two sides of the spread together, the Significator and mirroring card would face each other. For example, if reading the 8x4+4 GT (Figure 8a) with the Gentleman as the Significator, he/it is located in the third row and the sixth column. The mirroring card is then in same row in the third column (the Stars). If reading the 9x4 GT (Figure 8d) with the Lady as the Significator, she/it is located in the second row and in the sixth column. The mirroring card, the Dog, is then in the same row and in the fourth column. In a 9x4 GT, there will not be a mirroring card if the Significator is in the fifth column because that is the middle of the spread.

Read the Significator and mirroring card in a 2 Card Combination with the Significator in position 1 and the mirroring card in position 2 (It is irrelevant if the mirroring card is on the left or right of the Significator card).

Knighting

Knighting is used to uncover situations or issues that are buried or hiding from the querent or reader. They may be oblivious to underlying circumstances. Sometimes the querent doesn't want to admit things to the reader or even themselves. This is an opportunity to define or address these matters.

Knighting moves are similar to the moves of the knights on a chess board. Knighting can be done to the left, right, top, and bottom of the Significator, depending on where the Significator is located in the GT. There must be two rows or columns next to the Significator to knight in any given direction. Count two spaces away from the Significator (up, down, or to one side), then turn to the cards on either side of that spot (flanking cards or cards above and below). Those cards become a pair; that pairing becomes a 2 Card Combination. If they are vertically placed, use the top card in position 1 of a 2 Card Combination. If they are horizontally flanked, use the left card in position 1 of the 2 Card Combination.

Following is an example of knighting:

The Lady in the 9x4 GT (Figure 8d) is located in the second row and the sixth column.
- Above: Because of the Significator's location, there is not a second row above her. There will not be knighting above the Lady.
- Beneath: To knight beneath the Lady, count downward two positions to the Snake. The knighting cards are flanking the Snake. They are the Mountain and the Birds. Read these knighting cards as a 2 Card Combination (21+12).
- Left: To knight to the left of the Lady, count two positions to the left which is the Dog. The knighting cards on above and below the Dog are the Child and Clouds. Read those two cards as a 2 Card Combination (13+6).
- Right: To knight to the right of the Lady count to the right two positions which is the Ship. The knighting cards above and below the Ship are the Lilies and the Rider. Read those two cards as a 2 Card Combination (30+1).

Examples for the above pairings might read in the following way:

- Mountain and Birds: This 2 Card Combination is beneath the Lady and is about things that are actually happening in her life. This combination might represent serious blockages that are affected by communication or speech.
- Child and Clouds: This 2 Card Combination timeframe is in the past. It might be about a chronically depressed child in the life of the querent.
- The Lilies and the Rider: This 2 Card Combination is in the future. The querent could be receiving an acknowledgment they have been waiting for.

Nuances

There are several optional nuances that can add more meaning and layers to the Grand Tableau. However, these techniques are not built upon the card combinations that we have diligently and consistently used. Instead, we will be looking for clues or information the cards or card keywords may provide. Some of the more common nuances are listed below.

Cross Card

In the Grand Tableau, the Cross often represents a serious burden. It may be a place where the querent feels so stuck that their only option is to surrender a problem or situation to a higher power. Examine the flanking cards on either side of the Cross (without combining them as you usually do) to further understand where the querent is feeling stuck in their life. Those flanking cards may provide more insight into the proverbial "stuck between a rock and hard place" they may be experiencing.

Crossroads Card

In the Grand Tableau, the Crossroads (aka the Path) may provide extra insight into pressing decisions. It may reveal which directions the querent's choices could lead. After locating the Crossroads in the GT, one of the following methods can be used:

- The flanking cards on either side of the Crossroads are examined (without combining them) to see what kind of decision may be made. The querent's choices may lead to the card on the left or the card on the right.
- The two cards that are in the upper diagonal lines from the Crossroads, like a Y in the road, are

examined (without combining them). Another way to find these cards is to go up to the card that is one row above the Crossroads and then use the cards on either side of that card.
- The directions the roads lead on the face of the Crossroads card are examined. The roads usually lead two or three directions. Follow the direction of each road to determine where they lead and, as a result, where the querent's decisions are leading.

Scythe Card

The Scythe is about something cut-off or ending. Therefore, it is relevant where the tip of the blade is pointing because it is showing what exactly is ending. For example, in the Lenormand Silhouettes deck, the Scythe is pointing to the left. Look at the card on its left to determine what is cut-off or ending. In the Under the Roses Lenormand deck, the Sickle is used in lieu of the Scythe. It points up. Look at the card placed above it to see what is being cut-off or ending.

Relationships in the Same Row

When the Lady and the Gentleman are in the same row certain techniques may be used to further understand their relationship. If the Lady is the Significator, then locate the Gentleman. Is he to the left or the right of her? If he is to the left of her he's probably someone she knows because he's in the past. Depending on the surrounding cards, it may show if he's an ex. If the Gentleman is to the right of the Lady, then he may be a future relationship. The same would be true of the Lady if the Gentleman was the Significator. Note how far apart the cards are to determine the timing.

Pay attention to whether they are facing one another or have their backs to each other. If they are facing one another this may indicate that they are in agreement and if they face away from each other they may not be seeing eye-to-eye. The cards between their positions may show what is going on in an existing relationship.

Relationships Using Turning Points
If the Lady and Gentleman are not in the same vertical or horizontal line, there is an added technique called "turning points" that is helpful in understanding the foundation of a relationship. The turning points are paired in a 2 Card Combination to interpret the foundation of the relationship.

To use turning points, locate both the Lady and Gentleman. In relation to each other, figure out where the lines would have to <u>turn</u> to reach the other card. There will be two directions this can occur. These turning junctions are the cards that are combined into a 2 Card Combination.

For this example, we will use the 9x4 GT (Figure 8d). The Lady is in the second row and sixth column, and the Gentleman is in the third row and second column. First, follow the second row from the Lady to the second column where you must turn down to reach the Gentleman. So, the card above the Gentleman, the Ring (highlighted orange in Figure 8d), is a turning point for the combination. The Ring then becomes the first card of the 2 Card Combination because it is on the left. After that, follow the row the Gentleman is in to the sixth column where you must turn up to the Lady, the Key (also highlighted orange in Figure 8d). This then becomes the second card in the 2 Card Combination because it is on the right. The turning point on the left will always be in position 1 with the card on the right in position 2 of the 2 Card Combination. The Ring and the Key creates the combination of the turning points and is then interpreted.

Proximities
This is my adaptation. Should you elect to read proximities, it is important that you are comfortable

using the Grand Tableau and have a deep understanding of the deck. This will be a very individualized process. There is an existing technique in which the distance of certain cards in the Grand Tableau is used to make deductions (not interpretations). The most commonly used pairing in this technique is the Bear and the Tree. If the Bear is near the Tree, then it is presumed to indicate if the querent is dealing with health issues. However, in all of the previous methods and techniques provided, the cards need to be connected in some way in order to make that kind of conclusion, not merely plucked out of the GT. In other words, if they are not paired or somehow connected they won't have a relevant meaning. So why then, if the cards don't connect to the layout or other cards in some way, would you pair them? As an alternative, I recommend drawing conclusions from cards that are connected or in proximity within a 3x3 Grid. In this way, it is obvious if the Tree is affected by the Bear.

Eventually, the cards will develop relationships with each other that you can easily identify. As a result they play off of each other, even if they are not paired. Again, I look for them near each other in a 3x3 Grid that is within a GT. For instance, I know that if the Significator and the Snake are in close proximity it is never good. I see this as a troublesome person in the life of the querent or they are, in some way, their own worst enemy. While these are not traditional interpretations, they do provide some insight into what is going on in the life of the querent.

Record your thoughts about relationships in the cards before you implement making these types of connections in your readings. Some of the proximities that I look for are listed below. Again, they must be in the same 3x3 Grid surrounding the Significator.
1) The Snake and the Mice. This proximity indicates lots of problems. On one hand, the snake eats mice. On the other hand, there are a lot of mice *and* a snake! So, the snake needs to be removed and the mice need to be exterminated!
2) The Fox and the Snake. The fox is sneaky and he will outsmart the snake in the grass.
3) The Bear and the Mountain. The Mountain in this proximity indicates the presence of a serious issue that the querent may likely have a hard time getting over. However, the Bear is right at home on a mountain and has no problem navigating it. The querent may need a

reminder that they are, indeed, a bear in this situation.

4) The Snake and the Tower. This is an interesting one. When in proximity, these cards often represent a legal problem which may include a courtroom or prison, particularly if the Letter is around. In this situation, the Snake often represents a Judge.

The Grand Tableau Quick Reference Guide

1) Choose a Grand Tableau style.
2) Set your intention about your keywords, reading techniques, timeframe, and whether you will use houses.
3) Shuffle and lay out the cards. Locate the Significator. If it is in an undesirable location, note it, add cards if desired, or stop the reading and start another one.
4) Once you have a spread that works, interpret the theme of the reading using cornerstones.
5) Locate the Significator and follow the lines doing pair chains.
6) If there are other subjects you are interested in, repeat the process as if the 3x3 Grid were printed on a transparent sheet that can be moved over the top of the GT.
7) When drawing your conclusions pay attention to the timeline you have selected (weeks, months, etc.).
8) Read the destiny cards if applicable.
9) Check houses if using that technique.
10) Mirror the Significator.
11) Knight the Significator.

12) Add depth to the reading by adding any nuances you use and include your own observances.
13) If using your intuition, let that come through.
14) Make an overall assessment; summarize the reading.

Grand Tableau readings may convey a lot of information. Therefore, the querent should wait at least a month before doing another GT.

Homework:

Use the GT Quick Reference Guide. Practice the 8x4+4 spread (Figure 8a) or the 9x4 spread (Figure 8d). Each practice session will likely take more than thirty minutes (maybe even hours), so plan accordingly.

Write your interpretations and conclusions in your notebook.

Chapter 9: Suggestions

Mixing and Matching

It is possible to mix and match the cards from different Petit Lenormand decks if they are the same size (Figure 9a). Make sure the new blended deck has cards numbered from one to thirty-six. This is just plain fun to do!

Figure 9a

Companion Notebook

If you would like to create an organized Lenormand notebook include the following areas/tabs:
- Notes
- Lists and the 3x3 Grid
- Spreads
- Readings and Interpretations

You may want to include the following lists:

- Suggested Keywords or other traditional keyword lists
- PAMs
- Card Pairings
- People in the Cards
- Work in the Cards
- Money in the Cards
- Intimate Relationships in the Cards
- Card Attributes - Positive/Negative/Neutral
- The 3x3 Grid
- House Meanings
- Card Relationships for Proximities

Difficult Issues

Readings may reveal some very personal issues. However, your instincts are likely going to point you in the right direction, which may be the most important tool in your Lenormand tool box.

- Keep your boundaries and have healthy detachment about the querent.
- Remember to avoid reading about the 3 Ds! Death, divorce, and disaster are topics that should be referred to professionals, such as qualified readers and mediums, doctors, lawyers, or therapists.

- Be patient and gentle when bringing up topics that could emotionally jar a querent. If you are not pursuing professional readings, consider leaving those difficult topics alone. If you don't have the skills to deal with troublesome topics, you could actually aggravate the querent's experience of an issue so that they become unhinged.
- Since a lot of people have depression or psychological diagnoses of some kind, depression may be spotted in readings as well. Often the Clouds, Moon, and/or Mountain will be in proximity of a central card of a 3x3 Grid (Figure 6b). This is a sign that the depression is related to a specific issue. If those cards are surrounding a Significator then it is likely something the querent is dealing with personally. However, that is not definitive. Tread lightly and consider asking the querent if there is a problem. Remember, it isn't your job to manage another person's mental health (unless you are a qualified mental health professional). And, if you suspect the person isn't of sound mind, end the reading.
- The querent may expect a particular outcome from a reading and reject any other input than what they want to hear. I often explain that the

reading process opens up new possibilities and perspectives. If that doesn't change the situation, I explain that I cannot ethically tell them what they want to know (though I wish I could) because I have an obligation to interpret what I actually see.

- There is a situation that professional readers call "test the psychic." This is not the fun game you play at home with friends to see how psychically skilled someone might be. This is an unpleasant game in which a new querent sits before a professional reader and spends most of the reading time demanding they provide them with all the answers they are seeking without giving them any input. The querent may need to feel validated that the psychic is genuine, but this wastes a lot of valuable reading time. Sure, it feels good when we produce a ta-da! moment. However, that is more about ego than it is about a productive reading. Should you experience this when providing a reading, suggest to the querent that they might actually get more out of the reading if they become involved in it. Explain that you would like to have time to talk to them about core issues. On the other hand, if you do

quick back-to-back party or event readings, then ta-da! moments are very helpful.
- The querent, themselves, may be difficult. They may even be insulting. Suggest they see a professional or direct them elsewhere. The querent isn't likely to get help from the reading. Remember that you don't have to read for someone just because they've asked.
- Gently end a reading and offer a refund (if warranted) in any reading where you are not comfortable.

Appendix

Attached are extra copies of the Suggested Keywords list, the PAMs list, and the 3x3 Grid. They are here for your convenience and you are welcome to print a copy of them for your personal studies. Again, I am giving my permission to you to print a copy of the three documents in this appendix for personal use. Do not distribute copies in groups or publish them as your own works in any way. I ask that you respect the copyright of all my material, including images.

Suggested Keywords

1 Rider
News, Messenger, Visitor
2 Clover
Luck, Opportunities, Fortune
3 Ship
Travel, Moving, Vehicle
4 House
Home, Family, Property
5 Tree
Growth, Health, Longevity
6 Clouds
Unclear, Doubt, Depression
7 Snake
Betrayal, Seduction, Nemesis
8 Coffin
Transformation, Grief, Loss
9 Bouquet
Abundance, Gift, Romance
10 Scythe
Cut off, Ending, Harvest
11 Whip
Repetition, Arguments, Chemistry
12 Birds
Conversation, Chatter, Pairing
13 Child
Youth, Fun, Child, Sibling
14 Fox
Logic, Intelligence, Cunning
15 Bear
Overbearing, Heavy, Sturdy

16 Stars
Connectedness, Vision, Multitude

17 Stork
Beginning, Momentous Occasion, Announcement

18 Dog
Loyalty, Friendship, Pet

19 Tower
Perspective, Authority, Structure

20 Garden
Gathering, Networking, Event

21 Mountain
Challenge, Blockage, Endurance

22 Crossroads
Choice, Impasse, Direction

23 Mice
Annoyance, Problems, Anxiety

24 Heart
Love, Endearment, Empathy

25 Ring
Commitment, Agreement, Union

26 Book
Secrets, History, Reflection

27 Letter
Correspondence, Contract, Results

28 Man
Querent, Another Person, Important Person

29 Lady
Querent, Another Person, Important Person

30 Lilies
Harmony, Wisdom, Experience

31 Sun
Success, Vitality, Warmth

32 Moon
Cycles, Emotions, Shadowy

33 Key
Answers, Threshold, Destiny

34 Fish
Increase, Indulgences, Wishes

35 Anchor
Stability, Goals, Perseverance

36 Cross
Burdens, Stuck, Hopeless

© Kendra Hurteau 2018

PAMs
(Write your own keywords for each of the cards listed below)

1 Rider
2 Clover
3 Ship
4 House
5 Tree
6 Clouds
7 Snake
8 Coffin
9 Bouquet
10 Scythe
11 Whip
12 Birds
13 Child
14 Fox
15 Bear
16 Stars
17 Stork
18 Dog
19 Tower
20 Garden
21 Mountain
22 Crossroads
23 Mice
24 Heart
25 Ring
26 Book
27 Letter
28 Man - Querent, Significant Other
29 Lady - Querent, Significant Other

30 Lilies
31 Sun
32 Moon
33 Key
34 Fish
35 Anchor
36 Cross

© Kendra Hurteau 2018

| Influencing Thoughts of the Past

1 | Present Thoughts

2 | Influencing Thoughts in Future

3 |
|---|---|---|
| Position 2

Past Situation

4 | Position 1

Central Card Preselected or Random

5 | Position 2

Future Situation

6 |
| Influencing Past Happenings

7 | Present Happenings

8 | Influencing Future Happenings

9 |

3x3 Grid ©KendraK Hurteau

Bibliography

Books

Boroveshengra, Andy. *Lenormand Thirty Six Cards: An Introduction to the Petit Lenormand.* CreateSpace Independent Publishing, 2014

Dos Ventos, Marcus *The Game of Destiny - Fortune Telling with Lenormand Cards.* Nzo Quimbanda Exu Ventania, 2007

Dunn, Patrick. *Cartomancy with the Lenormand and the Tarot: Create Meaning & Gain Insight from the Cards.* Llewellyn Publications, 2013

George, Rana. *The Essential Lenormand: Your Guide to Precise and Practical Fortunetelling.* Llewellyn Publications, 2014

Katz, Marcus and Goodwin, Tali. *Learning Lenormand: Traditional Fortune Telling for Modern Life.* Llewellyn Publications, 2013

Louis, Anthony. *Lenormand Symbols: Exploring the Origins of the Images on the Cards.* Anthony Louis; Amazon Digital Services LLC, 2014

Matthews, Caitlín. *The Complete Lenormand Oracle Handbook: Reading the Language and Symbols of the Cards.* Destiny Books, 2014

Steinbach, Sylvie. *The Secrets of the Lenormand Oracle.* Createspace Publishing, 2007

Websites

British Museum. http://www.britishmuseum.org/research/collection_online/search.aspx

Donnaleigh http://www.divinewhispers.net/lenormandlessons.htm

Melissa Jo Hill. http://melissajohill.com

Merriam-Webster. https://www.merriam-webster.com/dictionary/Normand

Merriam-Webster. https://www.merriam-webster.com/dictionary/tableau

Learn Lenormand. http://learnlenormand.com/how-to-read-petit-jeu-lenormand/

Mary K. Greer. https://marykgreer.com/2013/07/21/the-petit-lenormand-tradition/

Under the Roses http://undertheroses.wixsite.com/undertheroses

U.S. Games Systems, Inc. https://www.usgamesinc.com/home.php

Card Decks

Das Spiel der Hofnung. G P J Bieling, 1800

Grand Jeu of Mlle. Le Normand, Grimaud, 1890

Mlle Lenormand Blue Owl. U.S. Games Systems Inc., 2011

No. 194115 Mlle Lenormand Cartomancy Deck of 36 Cards. Piatnik, date unknown

Thirty-Two Emblematical Cards (aka Viennese Coffee-Cards). Champante & Whitrow, 1796

Made in the USA
San Bernardino, CA
14 February 2019